M000305877

COCONUT

COCONUT

HOW THE SHY FRUIT SHAPED OUR WORLD

ROBIN LAURANCE

For Aileen

First published 2019

The History Press
The Mill, Brimscombe Port
Stroud, Gloucestershire, GL5 2QG
www.thehistorypress.co.uk

© Robin Laurance, 2019

The right of Robin Laurance to be identified as the Author of this work has been asserted in accordance with the Copyright, Designs and Patents Act 1988.

All rights reserved. No part of this book may be reprinted or reproduced or utilised in any form or by any electronic, mechanical or other means, now known or hereafter invented, including photocopying and recording, or in any information storage or retrieval system, without the permission in writing from the Publishers.

British Library Cataloguing in Publication Data.
A catalogue record for this book is available from the British Library.

ISBN 978 0 7509 9061 5

Typesetting and origination by The History Press
Printed and bound in Great Britain by TJ International Ltd.

CONTENTS

PROLOGUE

Imagine, if you will, a baronial hall with a huge open fire, burning logs from the estate. The logs crackle and spit onto the flagstone hearth. Deep leather armchairs and a couple of settees piled with cushions invite a pleasant dalliance – an invitation enhanced by the goblets and decanters of red wine that line the dark, Jacobean sideboard with its finely turned legs.

Let not your imagination be constrained by the passage of time, as into this convivial environment comes an unlikely collection of men and women, from times past and times present, who seemingly have little in common. Yet within minutes they are engrossed in each other's stories and the conversations sparkle in company with the energy of the open fire.

Here is William Hesketh Lever (Lord Leverhulme) the Bolton-born soap king of post-industrialised Britain. Next to him is a diminutive Vietnamese monk of uncertain age known to his followers as Dao Dua. Here too is William Wilson, a Scot aka Edward Price, who made candles for Buckingham Palace. Joining them comes Louis Fieser who had been an organic chemist at Harvard University where, with a degree of soul-searching, he invented napalm. Then comes the bearded German nudist August Engelhardt who as it happens studied physics rather than chemistry. He still has the look of a bohemian student about him, but in deference to his fellow guests, is wearing clothes. Imelda Marcos, the former first lady of the Philippines, is wearing shoes which she will have selected carefully and laboriously for the occasion: she had 1,600 pairs to choose from.

You may be tempted to avert your gaze from the disgraced man handcuffed to a prison warder. But examine this man without flinching: his story is shameful – but rather extraordinary. And if you don't recognise Captain William Bligh from *The Bounty*, no matter. What matters is that there was something about the 1789 mutiny on his ship you don't know, and he will certainly want you to know. He will have a satisfied-looking auctioneer from Christie's in tow. The French Enlightenment philosopher Voltaire will be espousing the merits of the British legal system to all the other Anglophiles in the room. From China come the white-gloved drivers of Shanghai's electric buses.

A cluster of devout Hindus from Kerala in southern India will indulge in quiet exchanges with Catholic farmers from the Philippines. Silversmiths from Antwerp and Augsburg will discuss their trade. A young John F. Kennedy in his naval lieutenant's uniform will be recalling his adventures in the South Seas during the Second World War. William Procter and James Gamble will turn up if their steamship makes it across the Atlantic, and Robert Pearce will speed through the Channel Tunnel from southern France where the world's largest experimental fusion reactor is under construction. Two friends, the sons of Errol Flynn and John Steinbeck, will reminisce about the Vietnam War.

The portly bespectacled French chemist Michel Chevreul, whose name is inscribed on the Eiffel Tower (together with those of France's seventy-two other leading scientists) will be recalling his life's story spanning 101 years – for anyone who will listen. And two horses without legs will clip-clop towards any hand offering sugar lumps. There will be many others too, but you will have no trouble in hearing above the general chatter what it is that these men and women have in common. And the goblets on that Jacobean sideboard provide the answer if doubts remain.

The wine goblets are fashioned from coconuts, and coconuts are what these people have in common. Coconuts have shaped the lives of some of them, while the others have used coconuts to shape profoundly the lives of others. No plant, nor any group of plants, has had a part in so many and such diverse areas of human activity as the venerable coconut. The current craze for coconut-based health foods and beauty products is just the latest manifestation of this remarkable plant's contribution to the lives of *Homo sapiens.* And doubtless in fifty years from now it will have become indispensable in those areas of human enquiry so far blind to the coconut's seemingly endless potential to be the answer.

I

SEX AND MUTINY

To botanists the coconut palm is the *Cocos nucifera*, a member of the *Arecaceae* or palm family. And the seed (or fruit) is strictly not a nut but a drupe, a fleshy fruit in the same family as the cherry and plum. *Cocos* probably comes from *coco*, the Spanish and Portuguese word for grinning face apparent in the face-like markings at the base of the hairy nut. Coconuts have been around longer than *Homo sapiens*, but where exactly the coconut palm began life is still a matter of conjecture amongst botanists and historians. The oldest coconut fossils, found in Gujarat, India's most westerly state, date back to the Eocene period some 37 million years ago – a period when dormice, hedgehogs and rhinoceroses, orchids and delicate lilies were already in evidence.

Writings in Sanskrit refer to coconut oils being used in Ayurvedic medicine 3,500 years ago. Coconuts appear again in the Hindu epic story of Shri Rama written in the Sanskrit language a thousand years later and known as the Ramayana. And the Arabic folk tales of *One Thousand and One Nights* include the seven voyages of Sinbad the Sailor, whose crew throw stones at monkeys who retaliate by throwing down coconuts – which the sailors promptly sell to finance their next voyage. (Monkeys, mostly pig-tailed macaques, are trained today throughout southeast Asia to assist with the coconut harvest, proving at least twice as efficient as their human counterparts at tossing the nuts to the ground, but troubling animal rights campaigners as they do so.)

The *Song of Solomon*, that celebration of love and sex which appears in the Old Testament of the Christian Bible and in the last section of the Hebrew Bible, the Tanakh, likens the woman's body to the coconut palm: 'How beautiful and how delightful you are, My love, with all your charms! Your stature is like a palm tree. And your breasts are like its clusters.'

Seafaring Arab traders likely carried coconuts from India to East Africa as long as 2,000 years ago. These mariners encountered coconuts as they traded with their Indian counterparts who sailed small, nimble *dhows* made from coconut-wood planking lashed together with coconut fibre (coir). The *dhow* was adopted by Arab merchant mariners themselves, and the boats continue to be used today, but made with modern materials. By the sixth century, these Arab merchants had brought the coconut to Egypt from East Africa. The celebrated Venetian merchants found coconuts lining the shores of the eastern tropics. In his 24-year exploration of Asia at the end of the thirteenth century Marco Polo came across coconuts first in India. He referred to them often in his diaries, *The Travels of Marco Polo,* writings that were to prove an inspiration for his fellow Italian explorer Christopher Columbus. Seemingly mindful of the arrival of coconuts in Egypt, Polo called his coconuts *Pharaoh's Nut* and reckoned each one was a meal in itself 'both meat and drink', he wrote.

During the Middle Ages when Kublai Khan was founding his Yuan dynasty in China and Genghis Khan his empire in

Coconuts on Hawaii. (Photograph by Brother Gabriel Bertram Bellinghausen via Wikimedia Commons)

Mongolia, coconuts were a prized rarity in Europe, encouraging nobles and leading churchmen to have them formed into cups mounted on gold or silver legs. Walter Kirkham had one. He had been elected Bishop of Durham in preference to King Henry III's half-brother Aymer de Valence. (Despite being an illiterate secularist, de Valence was already the Bishop of Winchester.) Kirkham, who became instrumental in the foundation of Balliol College at Oxford University, bequeathed his fine coconut goblet to his niece Isabella a year before he died in 1230, but what happened to the cup thereafter is a mystery. (Oxford's New College has a rare coconut cup decorated with a flowering hawthorn motif in silver. Oriel College has another. There are six altogether at Oxford and more in the colleges at Cambridge University and a particularly fine one at Harvard.)

Vasco da Gama, the Portuguese explorer, found coconuts on the east coast of Africa and the west coast of India and brought them to the Cape Verde islands in the Atlantic Ocean at the end of the fifteenth century. Coconuts continue to flourish there today. Da Gama's fellow countryman Ferdinand Magellan, encountered coconuts during his first circumnavigation of the globe in 1521 when, reduced to the point of starvation, he and his crew went ashore on the island of Guam. There they fed on coconuts and took plenty back on board. Antonio Pigafetta, a Venetian nobleman travelling with Magellan and documenting the voyage, wrote, 'As we have bread, wine, oil, and vinegar, so they get all these things from [coconut] trees … With two of these palm trees, a whole family of ten can sustain itself.'

Francis Drake found the Cape Verde coconuts a century later, and considering them a rarity, recorded the find in his journal:

> Amongst other things we found here a kind of fruit called Cocos, which because it is not commonly knowen with us in England, I thought good to make some description of it. The tree beareth no leaves nor branches, but at the very top the fruit

> groweth in clusters, hard at the top of the stemme of the tree, as big as severall fruite as a mans head: but having taken off the uttermost barke, which you shall find to bee very full of strings or sinowes, as I may terme them, you shall come to a hard shell which may holde a quantitie in liquor a pint commonly, or some a quart, and some lesse: within that shell of the thichnesse of halfe an inch good, you shall have a kinde of hard substance and very white, no lesse good and sweete then almonds: within that againe a certaine clear liquor, which being drunke, you shall not onely finde it very delicate and sweete, but most comfortable and cordiall.

The rarity value of the coconut was soon to pass. Sailors and adventurers took note of Marco Polo's observation that the nuts provided both food and water and started adding the nuts to their provisions for longer journeys. When the holds of the great sailing ships were full, coconuts were piled on the decks. The value of the young coconut lay in its ability to keep its water fresh and its meat edible for months on end. Polynesian, Asian and Arab seafarers had long used coconuts as reserve rations. In the Philippines an edict issued by Spain's Governor General Hurtado de Corcuera ordered each native to plant 200 coconut trees primarily to satisfy the thirst of the Galleon Trade's seafarers – generations of men who risked their lives operating the trade route between Mexico and the Philippines which began in 1565. Without coconuts, the exploration of our planet would likely have proceeded at a more tentative pace.

While the coconut proved an invaluable aid to the early merchant explorers, the nut did some travelling of its own. Coconuts float and not only do they float but their husk and tough shell can protect the seed for months. Carried on ocean currents and later on the ships of those early South Seas explorers, coconuts travelled the southern hemisphere, depositing their seed on beaches and shore lines from the South Pacific to the Indian sub-continent and on to South America.

The French Enlightenment philosopher Francois-Marie Arouet, better known as Voltaire, referred on one occasion to the ease with which coconuts took root in a variety of locations comparing this to the transplanting of one nation's laws and virtues to another. Describing the English as 'an unaccountable nation fond of their liberty', he observed how English laws were, in his words, on the side of humanity whereas French laws were against humanity. 'Why can't the laws that guarantee British liberties be adapted elsewhere?' he asked. 'There is no reason why coconuts should not flourish everywhere (which is not quite true) so let's start planting them now.'

When the direction of ocean currents failed to ensure dispersal, accidents with silver linings did the job. A Spanish brig, the 175-ton *Providencia* with a cargo of coconuts harvested in Jamaica, foundered soon after leaving Cuba on its way to Spain. Early on 9 January 1878 it finally ran aground on Florida's Atlantic Coast, scattering its cargo along the Sunshine State's shore line. Local residents rushed to the beach: 'I was greeted by the mate of the vessel, with a bottle of wine and a box of cigars, as a sort of olive branch,' wrote Will Lanehart, one of the men on the beach. 'There were 20,000 coconuts, and they seemed like a godsend to the people. For several weeks, everyone was eating coconuts and drinking wine.' Within a decade, the area was filled with palm trees and became known as Palm Beach.

As long as the palm can enjoy sandy soil, daytime temperatures above 25°C, high humidity, lots of rain and plenty of sunlight it can live for 100 years. Thriving on the ocean's edge, it has learnt to lean towards the water to absorb reflected light in addition to the direct light from the sun above. A young palm will start to produce fruit when it is five years old and as it reaches its prime of life will produce seventy-five fruits a year. (The palm itself can survive in less

The *Providencia* aground off the Florida coast.

than ideal conditions but is very unlikely to bear fruit.) The centre of the young nut contains the coconut water, not to be confused with coconut milk which is made from the coconut flesh by grating it and soaking it in hot water. The coconut cream rises to the top and can be skimmed off. The remaining liquid is squeezed through a cheesecloth to extract a white liquid that is coconut milk.

By the beginning of the sixteenth century, the coconut was already widely dispersed. It had sustained countless explorers, saved the lives of many, appeared in a variety of sacred texts and graced the mantle shelves of bishops, princes and the wealthy burghers of central Europe. The nut had been used to make drinking cups while the palm fronds had been used to provide roofing and baskets, and the coir – the husk of the nut – had been woven into rope and rigging for ships.

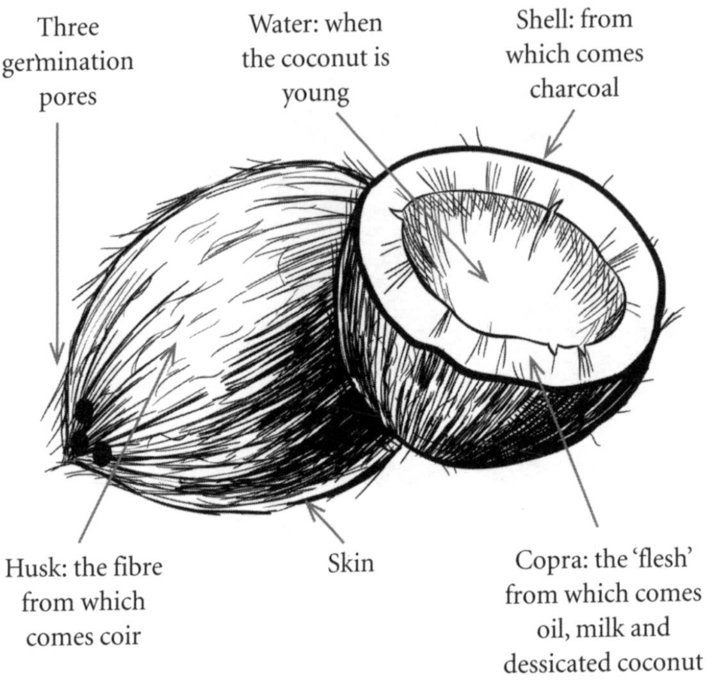

A cross-section through a coconut.

But this unsung hero of the plant kingdom had so far stepped only lightly on the human stage. In time, its footprint would stretch from the sandy tropical beaches of the South Seas to Britain's industrial heartland; to the bomb makers and chocolate makers of America; to Europe's goldsmiths and silversmiths; to the Hindus in India; to nuclear scientists in France; to smugglers from Mexico to London and onto supermarket shelves from Barcelona to Birmingham in Alabama. And it would be an unlikely catalyst for events that became firmly lodged in the annals of history.

One such event unravelled in the 1780s in the seas of the South Pacific. Those seafarers who had found salvation in the coconut persuaded ships' captains to carry coconuts as a matter of course. William Bligh, the stocky, blue-eyed, hot-tempered master of the three-masted Royal Naval vessel HMS *Bounty*, was one to take notice, carrying large reserves of coconuts wherever he went. His 1787 mission was no exception. Sanctioned by a still sane King George III, Bligh was to collect breadfruits from Tahiti in the South Pacific and transport them to the West Indies to provide cheap food for slaves. Bligh, an experienced sailor who had been the chief navigator on James Cook's third and final voyage on HMS *Resolution*, had set sail with a crew of forty-four Royal Navy seamen and two civilian botanists. Fletcher Christian, the 23-year-old son of a wealthy Cumbrian attorney was on board as the master's mate – one of two unpaid 'young gentlemen sailors'. Mr Christian, it turned out, was to have ideas above his station.

Having left Deptford on 15 October 1787, five months to the day after the first criminals to be shipped to Australia left Portsmouth (there were 736 of them in eleven ships), the *Bounty* almost immediately ran into bad weather and failed to reach Spithead until 4 November where it waited for final orders. Cautious officers at the Admiralty finally gave Bligh the go-ahead at the end of the month, but once again unfavourable winds trapped him in the Solent until two days before Christmas. Come the new year, they were at last on their way. Conditions on board were not as comfortable as they might have been. The great cabin had been converted into a giant hothouse for hundreds of potted breadfruit plants that were to be transported from Tahiti for re-planting in the Caribbean. This led to serious overcrowding below decks. Nevertheless, the journey began well enough with the irascible Bligh establishing particularly warm relations with his master's mate Fletcher Christian.

Bligh was a disciplinarian especially when it came to matters of hygiene and diet. The ship had to be kept spotless and the food prepared and served with the utmost attention paid to all-round cleanliness. The two cooks, Thomas Hall and his assistant William

Muspratt, responded to their captain's demands in good spirit, and the able seamen who took it in turn to clean the ship tackled their tasks with subordinate good grace. But all was not well above decks. John Fryer, the sailing master and Bligh's second in command resented, not unreasonably, Fletcher Christian's promotion to the rank of acting lieutenant and with it the role of the captain's number two. Then as the *Bounty* neared Cape Horn it ran into more bad weather. Storms drove the ship back time and time again, and after two weeks of gale-force winds, hail and sleet the crew were exhausted. Bligh admitted that the sea had beaten them and ordered a change of course that would take them to the Cape of Good Hope. Here they spent just over a month working on necessary repairs and re-provisioning before setting out across the Indian Ocean for Tasmania where the *Bounty* moored in Adventure Bay, a sweeping sheltered anchorage on the north-east corner of Tasmania's Bruny Island.

It was here that further signs of discord between Bligh and his men became evident with matters becoming worse on the final leg of the trip to Tahiti. John Fryer, whose nose had been put out of joint by Bligh's favoured treatment of Fletcher Christian, refused to sign the ship's accounts unless his captain provided a written appraisal of Fryer's overall competence on the journey so far. On top of that, the incompetence of the ship's surgeon, Thomas Huggan, who had been drunk for most of the trip, led to the death of James Valentine, one of the able seamen, and to a further decline in morale.

Once in Tahiti with the gathering of the breadfruit underway, spirits lifted and the *Bounty*'s crew enjoyed themselves ashore with the island's women. During the five-month stay, eighteen officers and crew contracted and were treated for venereal disease. Discipline began to falter. Fletcher Christian was amongst the officers harangued by Bligh for misdemeanours both real and imagined. Floggings became common. The potting and loading of the breadfruit took on a new urgency. After nearly twenty hedonistic weeks in their Polynesian paradise, it was time for the *Bounty*'s crew to make ready for the long journey to the Caribbean.

During the first two weeks of the voyage, tensions began to mount. Bligh would fly into rages not infrequently directing his wrath at Fletcher Christian. By the time they reached Tonga to replenish food and water supplies for the last time, the *Bounty* was not a happy ship. Christian led the party ashore to collect water but was constantly harassed by the islanders against whom they were unable to defend themselves because Bligh refused to let them carry arms. When the party returned to the ship with considerably less water than was necessary, Bligh tore at Christian calling him 'a damned cowardly rascal'.

Christian also took the flak for the loss of a small anchor which had been stolen by a group of unfriendly locals. By the time they set sail, Christian was angry and resentful. What happened next was to determine the fate of the *Bounty*'s mission. In addition to the ship's supply of coconuts, Captain Bligh had stashed away a private supply of his own, hiding them behind two of the ship's cannons. But his supply had mysteriously diminished in number, and Bligh pointed the finger at Christian, punishing the whole crew by cancelling their rum ration and halving their daily food allowance. It was the last straw. Christian, apparently in tears, sought refuge in his cabin. He did not brood for long. At about 5.15 a.m. on the morning of 28 April, Fletcher Christian went below, distributed arms to his companions and made for Bligh's cabin.

Bligh recorded events as they unfurled:

> Just before sun-rising, Mr. Christian, with the master at arms, gunner's mate, and Thomas Burket, seaman, came into my cabin while I was asleep, and seizing me, tied my hands with a cord behind my back, and threatened me with instant death, if I spoke or made the least noise: I, however, called so loud as to alarm everyone; but they had already secured the officers who were not of their party, by placing sentinels at their doors.

> There were three men at my cabin door, besides the four within; Christian had only a cutlass in his hand, the others had muskets and bayonets. I was hauled out of bed, and forced on deck in my shirt, suffering great pain from the tightness with which they had tied my hands.
>
> I demanded the reason of such violence, but received no other answer than threats of instant death, if I did not hold my tongue. The boatswain was now ordered to hoist the launch out, with a threat, if he did not do it instantly, to take care of himself.
>
> The boat being out, Mr. Hayward and Mr. Hallet, midshipmen, and Mr. Samuel, were ordered into it; upon which I demanded the cause of such an order, and endeavoured to persuade some one (sic) to a sense of duty; but it was to no effect: 'Hold your tongue, Sir, or you are dead this instant,' was constantly repeated to me.
>
> I continued my endeavours to turn the tide of affairs, when Christian changed the cutlass he had in his hand for a bayonet, that was brought to him, and, holding me with a strong grip by the cord that tied my hands, he with many oaths threatened to kill me immediately if I would not be quiet: the villains round me had their pieces cocked and bayonets fixed. Particular people were now called on to go into the boat, and were hurried over the side: whence I concluded that with these people I was to be set adrift.
>
> I therefore made another effort to bring about a change, but with no other effect than to be threatened with having my brains blown out.

With Bligh and eighteen men in the launch it settled dangerously low in the water. The nearest land was the island of Tofua about 35 miles to the north. Five hours after the mutineers first entered Bligh's cabin, Fletcher Christian ordered the rope holding the launch to the ship be cut. (See p.2 of colour section.)

> A few pieces of pork were then thrown to us, and some cloaths [sic], also the cutlasses I have already mentioned; and it was now that the armourer and carpenters called out to me to remember that they had no hand in the transaction. After having undergone a great deal of ridicule, and been kept some time to make sport for these unfeeling wretches, we were at length cast adrift in the open ocean.

The 23ft launch with no cabin was overcrowded, under supplied and had just two masts for sails and just two pairs of oars.

On board the *Bounty*, Christian threw all the breadfruit plants overboard and turned the ship towards the island of Tubuai some 520 miles south of Tahiti. They arrived a month later to a hostile reception and changed course for Tahiti. The *Bounty* was provisioned and with thirty Tahitians on board, headed back to Tubuai where they struggled to establish a community. Bligh meanwhile was putting his considerable navigating skills to good effect. Having reached Tofua and met natives who grew more aggressive by the day, Bligh decided their best option was to sail for Timor – a mere 4,000 miles to the west. As the launch pulled away from the shore, an angry mob caught hold of the stern rope and tried to prevent them from leaving.

Quartermaster John Norton jumped into the water to cut the rope free. He was immediately set upon, dragged out of the water and stoned to death while Bligh and his men, desperate for their own lives, escaped into deep water. But they were badly shaken and fearful of what lay ahead. And they had good reason. The 4,000-mile voyage met with wild storms and mountainous seas. Bligh endeavoured to keep up morale while the wet, wind, cold and strict rationing sapped the crew's strength.

'At night,' wrote Bligh in his journal, 'I served a cocoa-nut to each person for supper.' As the voyage progressed, the coconuts had to stretch a lot further: 'Our supper, breakfast, and dinner, consisted of a quarter of a pint of cocoa-nut [*sic*] milk, and the meat, which did not exceed two ounces.'

Yet within four of the toughest weeks imaginable with the small open launch tossed mercilessly and relentlessly by ruthless seas, and with a crew badly under-nourished and desperately short of sleep, Bligh had steered the battered launch through a gap in the coral of the Great Barrier Reef to the safety of a calm lagoon. The men, shattered and sickly but thankful to be alive, feasted on oysters and fruit. But fresh food and the opportunity to rest did not prevent tensions once again coming to the surface and Bligh argued bitterly with William Purcell, the *Bounty*'s carpenter. But Timor was still more than a thousand miles away and after three days in the lagoon, Bligh and his men headed out into the open sea again to face some of the harshest conditions of the whole voyage. Battered by huge seas and soaked to the skin, many of the men in the launch were near collapse when on 12 June, the coast of Timor came into view. Two days later with a crude union flag flying from the masthead, they sailed into the harbour at Coupang (now Kupang in West Timor), their epic voyage at an end.

From Coupang, Bligh and his party sailed to Batatvia (now the Indonesian capital Jakarta) and thence by commercial vessel back to England. Six of the men who had survived the terrible conditions at sea were in poor health, were terribly weak and did not make it home. Bligh was court-martialled for the loss of the *Bounty*, acquitted, promoted to the rank of post-captain, and given command of HMS *Providence*. With an escort vessel, Bligh and the *Providence* were despatched to Tahiti to fulfil the breadfruit mission the *Bounty* had failed to complete. The voyage was without incident. But the slaves in the West Indies did not like the breadfruit and refused to eat them.

A frigate was despatched to find the *Bounty* and arrest the mutineers. Fourteen of them were rounded up on Tahiti. At a court martial on board HMS *Duke* in Portsmouth six of them were found guilty of mutiny and sentenced to death. Of these, two received royal pardons and a third was given a stay of execution. Able seamen Thomas Burkett, Thomas Ellison and John Millward were hung from the yardarm of a guard ship in Portsmouth Harbour. Coconuts, greed and the cruel sea had taken a heavy toll. Yet Bligh was promoted to vice-admiral. He retired, and in 1817 died at the age of 63.

In 2002, almost 200 years after Bligh's death, the National Maritime Museum paid £71,700 for the coconut shell used by Bligh as a drinking cup during the epic forty-one-day journey to Timor from Tofua in the *Bounty*'s launch. The world's most expensive piece of coconut, it bears his initials and the words 'the cup I eat my miserable allowance out of'.

Christian meanwhile had sailed the *Bounty* to the Pitcairn Islands where it was broken up and, when all the useful pieces of timber had been collected for use in buildings on the island, set ablaze. The mutineers settled into a comfortable life until the Tahitians grew tired of the way the sailors were treating their women. In a series of well-planned attacks, Fletcher Christian and four of his comrades were murdered.

The fifty or so people who inhabit Pitcairn today – most of them direct descendants of the mutineers – lead a simple life as Seventh Day Adventists, having been converted by a visiting American missionary at the end of the nineteenth century. But just as the original community nearly destroyed itself fighting over sexual access to a dozen Polynesian women, so in 2004 the island was in the grip of a sex scandal. Seven men appearing before a New Zealand judge (appointed by the British government) were accused of molesting young girls on the island. The defendants argued that sex between young girls and much older men was all part of the island's culture, a claim supported by older women who said they needed the sex as much as the men did. But pleas of a culture having supported the men's behaviour over the centuries failed to move the judge. Six of the accused were found guilty and sent to prison. (One of the islanders, Tania Christian, 26, has long maintained that the prosecutions were part of a British plot to dismantle the community on Pitcairn and save the British taxpayers' money.)

A study of island records confirmed anecdotal evidence that most girls bore their first child between the ages of 12 and 15. Mothers and grandmothers were resigned to the situation, saying their own childhood experience had been the same; they regarded it as just a part of life on Pitcairn. One grandmother wondered what all the fuss was about. Not surprisingly the incestuous nastiness of the attacks (given Pitcairn's gene pool, it is inevitable that many of the victims and perpetrators were related) shocked the outside world. A community founded over two hundred years ago on psychological violence seemed unable to cast off its bullying past.

Nobody wants to move to Pitcairn these days. The population on Britain's smallest colony has been dwindling for years, and there are now fewer than fifty islanders left and locals are struggling to find new settlers. Only one application has been received to move to the island, even though the government provides all immigrants with a plot to build their own house and temperatures stay above 62°F (17°C) all year round.

Matters were made worse in 2016 when Michael Warren, a former Pitcairn mayor, was found guilty of downloading scores of hardcore child abuse images and films featuring children as young as 6. The legacy of trouble and violence sparked by a mutiny over stolen coconuts lives on. With just forty-two ageing islanders who busy themselves on the land, and make souvenirs for occasional tourists, the future for this tiny British outpost in the South Pacific, about halfway between Chile and New Zealand, looks a little bleak.

Across the South Pacific, coconuts had been sustaining a trade route that had its beginnings in the 1560s and which paved the way for globalisation. By the time Captain Bligh had lost the *Bounty* to Fletcher Christian and his fellow mutineers, trading galleons had been plying the ocean between Manila and Acapulco in New Spain for more than two hundred years. Miguel Lopez de Legazpi, a Basque seaman, colonial administrator and trusted lieutenant of Spain's Philip II (after whom the Philippines were named) was the first to cover the 9,000 miles from Acapulco to Manila during 1565 and in so doing to claim the Philippines for his king. Under orders from Luis de Vasco, the viceroy of New Spain, he made the journey in three months, arriving nearly half a decade after Magellan's unsuccessful Spice Islands adventures. He secured the Philippines for Spain and established a trade route across the Pacific that was to last 250 years. Sustained by coconuts – water from the younger green nuts, meat from the older mature ones and caulking made with coconut husk – the crews of the Manila galleon trade criss-crossed the Pacific between the Philippine capital and New Spain, carrying precious cargos of silks, silver, spices, ivory and diamonds. The passengers were a mixed bunch: Chinese traders, Spanish priests, Filipino labourers, nuns, merchants, condemned prisoners and colonial administrators. Food was scarce, conditions cramped and insanitary, and diseases of various sorts a constant companion. When passengers had to share space below deck with livestock, the journey became insufferable. The passengers were seasick, had animal urine and faeces to contend with, the smell was nauseating, and sleep came only with exhaustion.

The westerly journey was the easier of the two as the galleons sailed more or less due west on a line between the Equator and the Tropic of Capricorn, their sails filling with the northeast trade winds while the helmsman held a steady course that took good advantage of the north Equatorial current.

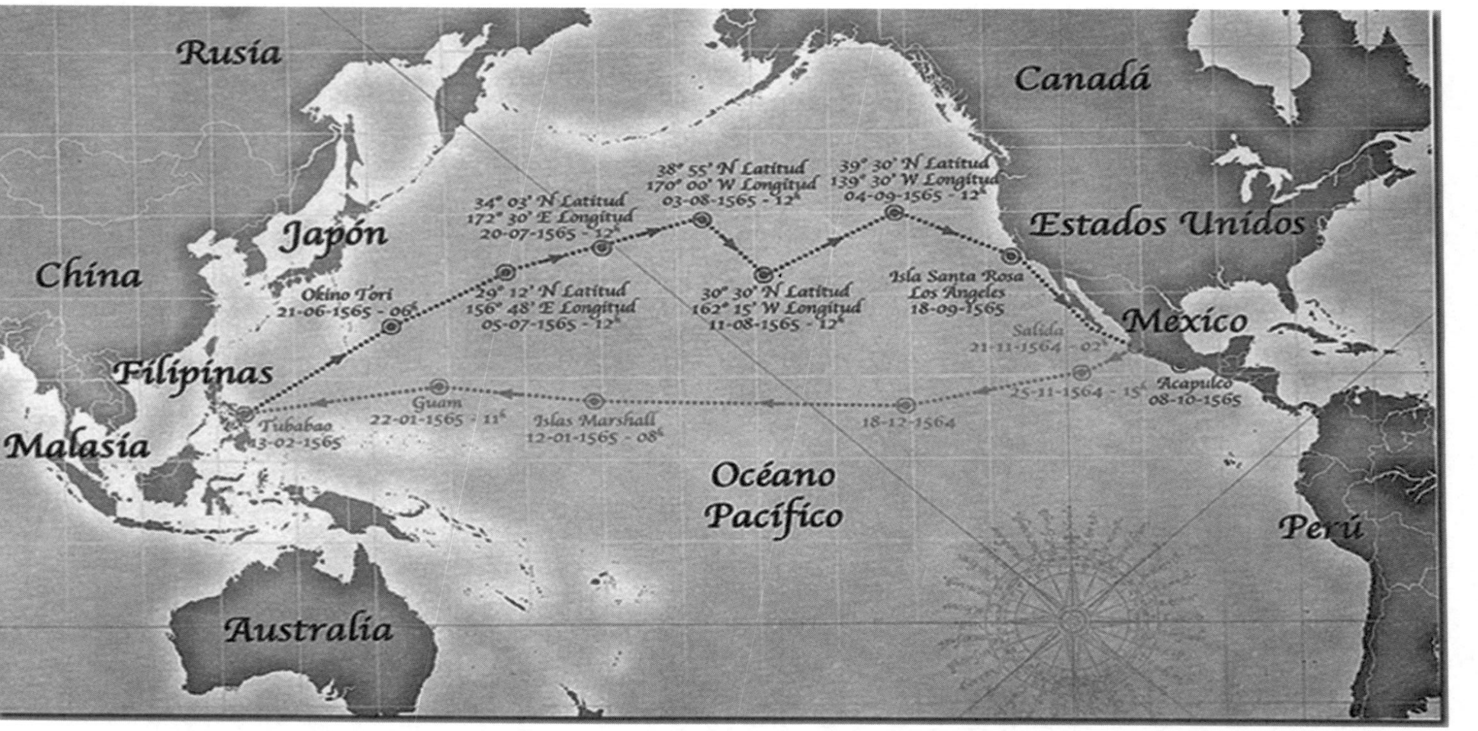

Map of the Manila Galleon Trade.

Silver was the most valuable of the cargos and there was plenty of it. Just twenty years before Legazpi's maiden voyage, huge deposits of the precious element had been found in the foothills of the Cerro Rico mountains in what is now Bolivia. Popular legend suggests an Inca searching for an escaped llama stopped to build a fire at the foot of a peak known as 'Potosi'.

The fire grew so hot that the very earth beneath it started to melt releasing a shiny liquid that ran in little rivulets across the parched earth. In April of 1545, the Spanish colonisers began work on a huge settlement at the foot of the mountains and began excavations in earnest. African slaves were imported to bolster the local labour force and mines began to take shape along the foothills for mile after mile. News of the find spread quickly and the colonial government had to impose licences for travel to the region. But this did not deter Spaniards determined to make their fortune from getting to Potosi by fair means or foul. Many took jobs on merchant ships heading for south America, and jumped ship when they docked. A trader at the time wrote: 'In every port where merchant vessels put down anchor, they jump ship and leave behind their duties and occupations, absenting themselves in anticipation of the liberties and uncertain riches of Potosi and the other mining centres.'

The warnings of uncertainties were well founded. The mines became home to thousands of rootless people forced to work under appalling conditions. The work was dangerous, causing numerous fatal accidents while hundreds more suffered silicosis pneumonia. To increase productivity, Francisco de Toledo, Peru's fifth viceroy who had taken charge of mining operations, issued a public order act requiring all African slaves over the age of 18 to work in shifts of twelve hours. But rather than coming to the surface at the end of a shift, the miners were to remain underground where they would work, eat and sleep for four months at a time. The death toll began to rise not least from the miners' contact with mercury in the smelting mills. By the end of nearly three centuries of colonial mining hundreds of thousands of lives were lost in the pursuit of the riches that had for so long lain hidden under the Andes.

For the mariners of the Manila galleons, sailing back in the other direction was more of a challenge and took much longer. It was Legazpi's pilot Fray Andres de Urdaneta who discovered the Kuroshio current. It took him north towards Japan where an easterly current and westerly winds took him on to Guam and then to the north of Hawaii and on to California where he turned south and followed the coast down to Acapulco. But the beginning of the voyage was particularly hazardous as the galleons had to negotiate dozens of tiny islands and their coral reefs in unpredictable and often violent winds. Many ships were wrecked soon after leaving port. More floundered in storms, while others were becalmed as disease and starvation decimated the crews. The *Nuestra Senora de la Concepcion*, under its inexperienced 22-year-old master, who happened to be the nephew of Manila's governor general, lost its way and was caught in a storm that broke its mast. Out of control, the ship was hurled onto a coral reef off the Mariana islands. Most of the 400 passengers and crew perished while its cargo of treasures was thrown into the sea. The site of the wreck is now overlooked by a golf course. Shards of Ming dynasty porcelain can still be found along the coastline. By contrast, the *San José* was found drifting off the Mexican coast more than a year after it left Manila. Every one of the passengers and crew had died either of starvation or disease. Rotting corpses, bundles of silk, spices, porcelain – much of it still in one piece – languished in what had become a ghost ship, its hull creaking as it swayed in the gentle swell.

The galleons were built at a shipyard in Manila Bay. Tropical hardwoods such as lauan, dangan and teak – and they were very hard – formed the decking and the hull. So tough were the hulls that pirate ships, including those of the British Navy, found their cannons did little damage. The shipwrights made the galleons' rigging – the sheets for the sails, the halyards, the shrouds – from the woven husk of coconuts and made the all-important caulking from a combination of husk and pili nut oil. Native and Chinese craftsmen meticulously worked the caulking into every seam between the planks and then sailed with the ships to manage the inevitable leaks: they hardly had a moment's rest.

From Manila the galleons carried silks, jade, tea, porcelain, nipa palm raincoats and furniture from China; cinnamon, cloves and nutmeg from the Spice Islands; ivory from Cambodia; ebony, sapphires and rubies from Burma; diamonds, cotton goods and curry powders from India, and from the Philippines themselves, coconut products, cotton stockings and petticoats, and jewellery made by local artisans. The galleons' manifests show that a third of all the silver mined in New Spain made its way to Manila often as ballast in the ships' main hold. The Philippines, their Asian neighbours and China became dependent on these shipments of silver to trade. With the silver came missionaries, manufactured goods from Europe, drugs, lace, fruits, horses and cattle. Such was the demand from the sailors for coconuts, for their fresh water and husk, that in 1642, nearly one hundred years after the galleon trade began, the Spanish governor general in Manila, Sebastian Hurtado de Corcuera, ordered every native Filipino to plant 200 coconut palms – an edict that set the Philippines on the road to becoming the world's leading producer of the nut.

2

ADVENTURES IN THE SOUTH PACIFIC

Just over thirty years after the Unionists had won the Civil War in America the country was at war again – this time not with itself but with the Spanish. The Americans' first target was the Spanish regime in Cuba. But Cuba was just the start. There were bigger fish to be had on the other side of the Pacific.

The Philippines had become a Spanish colony way back in the sixteenth century. It was a colonial adventure that was about to come to an end. On a May morning in 1898 Commodore George Dewey on his flagship the cruiser USS *Olympia* led a US naval squadron into Manila Bay and destroyed Admiral Montijo's anchored Spanish fleet in a leisurely morning engagement. Within six hours every Spanish ship had been sunk. Seven American seamen were wounded. Dewey returned a hero, was promoted to Admiral, and at a reception for him and his wife two years later was showered with unrestrained, extravagant praise:

> On a bright May morning two years ago there came from out (of) the ocean mist an untried naval squadron, mirroring in the rippling waves the flag of the mistress of the Western world, the lustre of whose shining stars has never been dimmed by dishonour or defeat, seeking in Manila Bay the naval pride and power of Spain … from out of the din and smoke of battle there arose a colossal figure, calm and majestic, cool and self-reliant … a naval hero, the splendour (sic) and brilliancy of whose achievement have written on the eternal tablet of fame … the immortal name of Admiral George Dewey.

So gushed one Josiah T. Settle, a lawyer and member of the Mississippi House of Representatives.

Manila itself was occupied by US troops by August, and at the Treaty of Paris in 1898, the Philippines with Manila as its capital, were ceded to the United States, at a cost to the Americans of US $20 million. The country did not gain full independence again until 1946 after the American and the Philippine armies had fought side by side to rid the country of the Japanese troops who had invaded the country in 1942 during the Second World War.

By acquiring the Philippines at the end of the nineteenth century, America had secured its supply of coconuts which it needed for the manufacture of soap. The Philippines, consisting of more than 7,000 islands, most of them uninhabited and hundreds not even named, has coconuts a plenty. And on land reclaimed from the sea in the bay of Manila, the graveyard of that routed Spanish fleet, there is a building that eloquently and extravagantly celebrates the coconut. Filipinos know it as the Coconut Palace: the cynical amongst them refer to it as Imelda's white elephant.

Imelda Remedios Visitacion Romualdez y Trinidad was born in Manila in 1929. She was one of five children. Her family were landowners. Her uncle Norberto was a supreme court judge. Imelda was blessed with good looks and a decent singing voice, both of which she put to good use, modelling, entering beauty contests and singing traditional Filipino love songs: she even recorded an album with the local pop diva Papin.

Early in 1954 she met a lawyer and Congressman called Ferdinand Marcos. The whirlwind romance lasted eleven days. Marcos told Imelda how much he loved her, sent her roses, proposed, but omitted to tell her that he was living with another woman. Carmen Ortega was another beauty who had been Marcos' live-in lover for two years. Quite how Marcos managed to spirit Carmen out of the house remains a mystery. But banish her he did, taking Imelda for his bride in a civil ceremony on Good Friday in 1954. The couple then got married again in a glamorous church wedding on May Day a fortnight later. But it was a union that would be despised for its excesses and shamed for its malpractice.

Within eleven years of their marriage, Marcos was elected president and there began twenty years of dictatorial self-serving misrule, tainted by brutality, corruption, cronyism and embezzlement of taxpayers' money on an unprecedented scale. Mrs Marcos joined in the fun, going on extravagant shopping trips to Paris, New York and London where her spending on clothes knew no bounds. Her celebrated collection of shoes ran into the thousands. (765 pairs are currently on show in the Marikana Footwear Museum.) On her shopping trips she managed to collect a coterie of unsavoury 'friends' which included Richard Nixon, Muammar Gaddafi, Fidel Castro and Saddam Hussein.

But it was coconuts that led to the greatest upset during her years of flamboyant extravagances. In 1978 the first lady summoned Francisco Mañosa, her country's most celebrated architect. On her world travels, she told him, her hosts would put her up in splendid government guest houses that through their construction and artefacts celebrated that country's culture. Now she wanted a similar guest house in Manila celebrating the nation's rich natural resource – its coconuts. And there was no time to spare. Cardinal Sin, the head of the Catholic Church in the Philippines, had persuaded His Holiness Pope John Paul II to visit early in 1981, and who better to be the first foreign dignitary to set foot in her new guest house than the Pope himself.

The first lady was as wily as she was impatient. She knew that the government's agriculture ministry had just sanctioned the felling of all coconut trees over the age of 60.

She had all the raw material she could possibly need. The idea of reflecting the nation in the new building suited Mañosa too: 'Architecture,' he says, 'must be true to itself, to its land and to its people.' The idea of using coconut suited his philosophy. But for Mañosa and his team of architects and designers, the first lady was just a few years premature in her demands as the technology for using coconuts in every part of the proposed building was not yet tried and tested. Plans and drawings were made which would provide plenty of scope for the interior designers but rather less for the structural engineers. Nevertheless the palace would celebrate the coconut palm inside and out, upstairs and down.

The building that emerged is hexagonal in shape and fashioned in the style of Castilian houses of the Spanish period. The roof tiles were made from the bark of the palm trunks, and the pillars from coconut timber. The grand doors of the main entrance are covered with small pieces of nut shell. Once inside, guests pass either side of a large circular table richly inlaid with more tiny diamond-shaped pieces of nut above which hangs a chandelier of 101 lights held in coconut cups. Underfoot, coconut parquet, sealed and polished, leads the way to the state dining room with its grand table for twenty-four guests. (See p.9 of colour section.)

Constructed of narra, an indigenous hard wood, its surface is inlaid with 47,000 pieces of coconut shell – dark pieces from older nuts and lighter pieces from younger ones – replicating the design of the Barong Tagalog, the national dress.

Each piece of shell is no more than an inch in length, needing the tiny, nimble fingers of sixty unusually patient children to put them in place. Today their work is surveyed by another youngster.

A portrait of the last king of Manila, Rajah Sulaiman, gazes with the innocence of youth across the table. He assumed the throne at the age of 13 and died four years later having failed to repel the Spanish.

Upstairs in the Coconut Palace – Imelda thoughtfully had the carpet on the grand staircase made of non-slip matting made from coconut coir – the first lady introduced an extraordinary wallpaper made of guinit, sheaths taken from the ribs and base of coconut fronds. Light brown in colour and with a rough surface, the walls of the palace became dark and heavy. Along corridors with coconut under foot and cladding on the walls, Imelda would lead her favoured guests to the Zamboanga room – her after-dark *piece de resistance.*

Named after the country's most prolific coconut region in the south of Mindinao, the bedroom is all coconut: the floor, the ceiling, the wallpaper, the king-size, four-poster bed with its carvings by Napoleon Abueta, and the ornate bedside lamp. The en suite bathroom has laminated tiles of coconut and a grand hexagonal mirror framed in coconut.

Sitting on the toilet, guests were surrounded by dark coconut tiles.

Costing around US $10 million the palace was opened with much razzmatazz in 1981 just in time for the visit of the Pontiff. But Mrs Marcos was in for a shock. When the Pope laid eyes on the guest house he declared it far too opulent in a country with so much poverty, and to Imelda's lasting chagrin His Holiness decided instead to stay downtown with his outspoken cardinal. (On one occasion Cardinal Sin likened himself to Jesus, saying that, seated between the Marcoses, he felt that he was being 'crucified between two thieves'.) If the stench of raw sewage on the breeze off the bay was anything like it is today, the Pope would have had further reason to take shelter with the cardinal. (George Hamilton, the American screen and television actor, mere mortal and close friend of Imelda's, was given the Zamboanga room when he stayed.)

The Pope, extricated from the clutches of the Marcos pair, got on with the business at hand. He beatified the first Philippine martyr Lorenzo Ruiz, denounced masturbation as a mortal sin and moved on to Guam on the next leg of his tour. The palace became the office of the Philippines' thirteenth vice president Jejomar Binay but his successors, like the Pope, considered it too showy.

In 1986, five years after the Pope's visit and with opposition demonstrators on the streets, the Marcos duo were finally forced to flee Manila twenty years into their reign of deceit, embezzlement and abuse of human rights. But Ronald Reagan, then the US President, had forged a relationship with them, while his Secretary of State George Schultz and Defence Secretary Caspar Weinberger had both reluctantly supported Marcos to ensure the tenure of vital US military bases in the country.

So the American Air Force whisked the couple and their family first to Guam and then on to Hawaii where they were greeted by US officials. Had they wished to send messages home after settling in, the US Postal Service would have been happy to oblige. On the Hawaiian island of Molokai, just a short hop from Honolulu, there is a post office on Puupeelua Avenue near the airport where postmaster Garry Lam does a brisk business in mailing coconuts – and little else. He invites senders to write the address and their own messages on the nuts and then attaches an array of colourful stamps to cover the postal cost, usually between $10 and $15 depending on the weight. (Customers are advised to choose water-free mature nuts which are much lighter.) Coconuts mailed to addresses in mainland America take about four days; the international service is more expensive and takes longer. But for Mrs Marcos, Ronald Reagan would probably have waived the charge.

Ferdinand Marcos died in Honolulu in 1989 after a prolonged illness. His body was returned to his home country, embalmed and displayed in a glass box. It has since been interred, after a great deal of argument and public outcry, in Manila's National Heroes' Cemetery. The burial was accompanied by a twenty-one-gun salute.

Imelda was eventually allowed to return home too, and in 2010 at the age of 81, even won a seat representing Ilocos Norte in the House of Representatives. It was the district her late husband had represented when he first entered Congress sixty-one years earlier, and where their daughter Imee is the provincial governor.

In November 2018 a special court in Manila found Mrs Marcos, by then 89, guilty of corruptly stashing away US $200 million in a Swiss bank account. She was sentenced to 77 years in prison – a sentence against which the former first lady has launched an appeal. Given the time such appeals take to run their course, she can look forward to a few more years of guilty freedom.

For the Philippine coconut industry, the Marcos legacy is decidedly mixed. He pulled the various state coconut organisations together under one roof calling the new outfit the Philippine Coconut Authority. Its remit – to strengthen the industry by providing support and advice to the farmers – has met with limited success. Some farmers receive free or subsidised fertiliser and free seedlings, but laws governing the size of land ownership have restricted plantations to an area too small to farm efficiently, and many farmers live in poverty.

But Marcos had a special treat in store for his struggling and neglected coconut farmers – a treat which turned sour and further clouded his legacy. The Coconut Levy Fund he created was a tax imposed on growers, the money from which was supposed to be ploughed back into the industry to improve productivity. Two of the president's cronies had other ideas. They creamed off a huge proportion of the fund for themselves, investing the money in ventures with nothing to do with coconuts and everything to do with personal gain. Farmers were quick to point an accusing finger at Eduardo Cojuangco Jr. Cojuangco was known as one of the 'Rolex 12', the group of untrustworthy millionaires nearest to Marcos. The farming community accused him of diverting their funds into the brewer San Miguel in which he gained a controlling stake and eventually became chairman. In a land raked by poverty, Cojuangco is said to be worth more than a billion US dollars. *Forbes* magazine has ranked him amongst the world's 1,000 richest people. Philippines President Rodrigo Duterte had promised the electorate that monies from the fund would be returned to the farmers. A year into his presidency the farmers were still waiting.

Ever since coconuts served as an integral part of the Manila galleon trade which brought wealth to the Spanish colony in the sixteenth and seventeenth centuries, the nut has retained its usefulness and has become vitally important to the economy of the modern independent nation. Today there are 3.5 million coconut farmers in the Philippines who, in 2016, produced 35 per cent of the country's exports in value terms. They tend some 330 million palms which have produced on average 15 billion nuts over the past three years. And that gave the Philippines 59 per cent of the world's coconut exports.

Yet 60 per cent of farmers live below the poverty line. Access to land and lack of secure tenure is one of the main drivers of poverty and inequality in the Philippines. Plantations are small, by government decree, which makes them inefficient. Few have any machinery to speak of. Most farmers are poorly educated and are beholden to greedy and devious traders who play on the farmers' weaknesses. The weather is fickle; the younger generation leaves the countryside for work and a brighter life in the cities; terrorists of various hues plagued the south (the most important coconut region) and corruption continues to blight the country and its farmers. In 2017 the head of the Philippines Coconut Authority no less was relieved of his position amidst allegations of corrupt activities involving coconut timber. Avelino Andal ('Billy' to his colleagues) who was appointed by President Duterte himself was suspended after spending less than six months in the job.

As youngsters look for work in the cities, the average age of coconut farmers in the Philippines has passed 50. Hernani, who is 57, has a 1-hectare coconut plantation in North Cotabato on the southern island of Mindinao. His 100 palms each produce about fifty coconuts a year. He is fortunate. He can still find young labourers locally to do his picking. They climb the trees in the early morning to avoid the searing heat of the day, first cutting shallow grooves in the trunk to make the barefoot climbing easier. Hernani's 36-year-old daughter who teaches at the local school, helps collect the coconuts as they hit the ground. She loads them onto a bullock cart which takes them down to the house where what passes for a road begins. Here the load is transferred to a jeepney, a stretched jeep invariably garishly painted with religious or nationalistic themes, and with bench seats inside but no glass in the windows. The jeepney takes the coconuts to the trader's warehouse, spilling nuts from the glassless windows as it weaves and bumps along the track. (See p. 14 of colour section.)

The traders, many of whom belong to families of Chinese immigrants, clearly exercise a stranglehold over the farmers. This is partly as a result of transport facilities badly in need of modernisation. Farmers currently using their buffaloes, tricycles and jeepneys, could bypass the traders and increase their profits if communications were better. On top of which traders tend to hoard supplies until their customers scream, when the price shoots up. But not an extra peso goes to the farmers. And the farmers are told by the traders that stocks are plentiful which, although often not true, gives the traders all the bargaining chips.

Pedro is 73. He has 400 coconut palms on 10 hectares in Panabo on the edge of the Davao metropolitan area of Mindinao. He has his three unmarried sons to help him. Pedro Jr, the eldest at 36, does the climbing to cut down the nuts – a job he has been doing since he was a child. His youngest brother drives the carabao (bullock) cart. They harvest every three months collecting around 4,000 coconuts in a twelve-month cycle.

The boys, none of whom had an education beyond primary school, share a single room in a home, built from local timber, which has no television or computers. They have mobile phones to communicate with the traders who buy their nuts, and they share a single motorbike, the family's only means of motorised transport. And that is the sum total of the mechanised support they have on the farm. But Pedro has been wise. Under his palms he has planted a variety of vegetables and several hundred banana palms, enough for the family with plenty left over to sell at market.

Eduardo's is a different story. He came to coconut farming in Mindinao from growing rice up north on the family farm in Luzon. 'God planned for me to do this,' he says. If God did the planning, Eduardo certainly did a good job executing the plan. He represents the minority of coconut farmers who bring business acumen to plantation management. The best profits come from the sale of seedlings so he makes that his priority. He won't have people climbing trees because the danger involved is not worth the risk. Youngsters are not interested anyway and the older men are slow and often hungover from too much palm toddy the night before.

So he hires pickers with bamboo poles topped with a small sickle. (He has learnt to keep his distance when picking starts after a nut landed on his head. 'I saw a lot of stars,' he recalls.) A single piece of bamboo reaches the nuts on dwarf palms but two or three lengths lashed together are needed to reach the taller variety. It would, Eduardo says, be more practical to train monkeys to do the picking, but he worries about the opposition from animal welfare groups. (Pigtailed macaque monkeys are trained and chained on plantations in Thailand.) A mechanised cherry picker would be ideal if he could afford one. But banks are loath to make loans available to coconut farmers who have no fixed income, not least because of unreliable weather patterns.

As it is, teams of local freelance pickers with their own buffalo carts and lengths of bamboo do the picking. A team of three can harvest between 1,000 and 1,500 coconuts on a good day. Wind makes picking more demanding as the bamboo rods become difficult to control – especially when two or three lengths are lashed together. And strong winds are a feature of the Philippine climate.

Fifty per cent of Eduardo's nuts qualify as sellable seedlings. If the price for copra is high, he opens the nuts and dries the copra which he sells to the highest bidder. And he burns the nut shell to produce charcoal using discarded husk as fuel. With what's left he makes fertiliser using the African night crawler, the most efficient of the composting earthworms, to do the pulverising. When the price of copra drops he sells the nuts whole to traders. His small house on the plantation is made of coconut timber. His wife cooks their vegetables in coconut milk and they both drink coconut water. They buy soap made with coconut oil and Eduardo puts virgin coconut oil on his skin. He says the twenty-three years he has been on the plantation have been the most exciting he could imagine.

Manuel Chu has had his excitements managing a large plantation for the Ayala Corporation, the country's oldest conglomerate with interests that range from coconuts to insurance and telecommunications. The single-storey office building we meet in was once a fine two-storey colonial building until the New People's Army burned it down, slaughtering his herd of cattle for good measure at the same time. The New People's Army (NPA) is the 4,000-strong armed wing of the Philippine Communist Party, a revolutionary guerrilla group active in the Philippines since the 1960s. Extortion is the modus operandi of the NPA. Manuel's crime was to stand up to the group, refusing to meet their demands for cash. He last received a letter 'asking for financial support' in 2016. He declines to say whether or not he acceded to the demand, but now has a detachment of seven armed military personnel protecting his farm.

Muslim separatists claiming allegiance to Islamic State, the NPA communists and criminal gangs have plundered and murdered their way through Mindinao since the early 1970s. As recently as 2018 law enforcement officers pointed the finger at a ruthless gang known for kidnapping and demanding ransoms when a bomb killed soldiers and civilian bystanders on the island of Basilan just off the Mindinao coast.

Manuel's farm has a total of 56,000 palms which produce some 25,000 nuts per day although extensive dry periods can reduce the output by 50 per cent. While the NPA presents an ongoing, large-scale threat, small time crooks who steal his coconuts under cover of darkness present a further challenge. He no longer cuts shallow steps into the trunks of the trees which made the climbing for legitimate pickers easy, preferring instead to employ pickers with bamboo poles and sickles on the end.

Working in teams of four – two pickers, one loader and one cart driver – his harvesters are expected to fill four trailers each with 1,500 nuts in a single day shift for which they are paid the minimum wage of 335 pesos (£6). Once harvested, the husks of the coconuts are removed by labourers protected from the sun by a rudimentary screen of leaves and twigs bound together. Their darkened sun-baked skin glistens with beads of sweat as they plunge the nuts onto a rusty blade secured in a wooden base. Once free of the husk, the nuts are cut in half and laid to dry over a fire fuelled by the discarded husk. There is not a single piece of machinery in sight. It falls to a second worker sitting cross-legged above the burning husk to scoop the copra out of its shell. This copra is sold to local mills who extract the oil; the husk goes to the makers of geotextiles and fibres, and the shells are turned into charcoal.

Charcoal has become big business for plantation owners, and local entrepreneurs have jumped on the bandwagon. One such company, BF Industries, produces industrial quantities of activated coconut charcoal – 'activated' by passing steam through the crushed powdered charcoal at high temperatures. It is the adsorbing properties of this treated charcoal that makes it ideally suited to a wide range of uses from trapping unwanted gases and filtering water for drinking, to the treatment of overdoses and the storage of electricity.

Tata Fernandez is the son of BF president Bonifacio Fernandez and vice-president of operations. His charcoal has found export markets in Japan, China, Belgium, Germany and Holland and in the world's leading gold mining countries. Gold cyanide is the result of extracting the gold from its ore and then leaching it with cyanide as the solvent. The suspension of gold cyanide is passed through a filtering system which consists of activated coconut charcoal. The charcoal adsorbs the gold but not the cyanide, and electrolysis then separates the gold from the charcoal. While gold mining has claimed the new high-value spot for activated carbon, water purification remains the largest market for the charcoal. It is used both industrially and domestically. Activated carbon made from coconut shells has pores in the micropore range, i.e. smaller than a pin's head. Almost 90 per cent of the surface area of coconut shell activated carbon exists as micropores. These small pores match the size of contaminant molecules in drinking water and therefore prove very effective in trapping them.

Gas masks remain an important end product for the charcoal, continuing the trend which began with attempts to deal with poisonous gas attacks in the First World War. Fernandez supplies civil and military mask manufacturers in China and in Japan where medical researchers are investigating the use of coconut charcoal in filters for kidney dialysis machines, while other customers use coconut charcoal in high capacity batteries and mobile phone capacitors.

Successful though the company has become, BF Industries has not been immune to the extortion racket operated by the New People's Army (NPA). Fernandez says he has to judge how serious the extortionists are and how likely they are to carry out their threats. He paid up on one occasion but now takes a much tougher line. It is not a subject he cares to discuss at any length. But he remains mindful of the NPA attack on a food packaging plant in 2017 which burnt the place to the ground. (When President Duterte was mayor of Davao, the centre of the coconut industry on the southern island of Mindinao, he was accused of having friends in the NPA, and even suggested that the people might think of payments to the NPA in the same way they think about payments to the tax authorities. The president's daughter Sara became the city's mayor in 2016 with her brother Paolo continuing in the role of vice-mayor.)

While Tata Fernandez produces coconut charcoal on an industrial scale with a well-educated workforce and modern machinery, most of the country's coconut farmers produce their own charcoal the hard way. They remove the husk and cut the nuts in half to dry the copra. The dried copra is extracted from the halved nuts and set aside to dry further. Then a hole is dug and a fire made with the nuts' discarded husk. The nut halves are laid on the fire and covered with pieces of banana trunk and a light covering of earth to control the combustion. The nut shells burn slowly, emitting a thick white smoke which after about six hours turns a blueish grey when more earth is added to starve the fire of oxygen. A day later the fire has died and the farmer has his charcoal.

Charcoal kilns have been introduced by the Philippines Coconut Authority, but they are expensive and require the farmers to make a substantial investment for which there is no state subsidy. And the farms are so small after the enforced break up of plantations, the banks are not interested in lending. They will lend to cooperatives, but in a nation of individuals the cooperatives rarely work: it goes against the grain. The inability to invest hampers growth and efficiency, and additionally the weather in this region of the South Pacific presents its own challenges. While year-round temperatures and rainfall generally provide ideal coconut growing conditions, exceptions in the weather pattern wreak havoc. *El Nino* which brought a drought in the first half of 2016 caused a huge loss in the quantity of copra (the flesh within the nut) which hit farmers hard and put a dent in the country's foreign earnings. But the greatest hazard comes from the Pacific typhoons to which the Philippines are particularly prone, added to which the country lies in an area of intense seismic activity being located along the border of two tectonic plates on 'The Pacific Ring of Fire'. Twenty-three active volcanoes are monitored day in, day out.

However nothing prepared the country and its coconut farmers for the events of 2013. Twenty-four tropical storms had swept across the Philippines in the first ten months of the year. Then on 4 November satellites began picking a tropical depression forming to the south-east of Guam. At first, there appeared to be nothing out of the ordinary. The satellite images were relayed to meteorological offices throughout the region including the Philippines own Atmospheric, Geophysical and Astronomical Service whose radar stations were getting their first indications of the low energy depression. But something unusual was happening. By 5 January, the depression had intensified and had come to the interest of the Joint Typhoon Warning Centre run by the US military in Hawaii.

By the end of 5 January what started as a mild depression twenty-four hours earlier had developed into a storm. The job of naming the storm fell to the Japanese Meteorological Agency, the official Regional Specialised Meteorological Centre for the western Pacific. They called it Haiyan. By 6 November, Haiyan was spinning toward the territory for which the Philippine Atmospheric, Geophysical and Astronomical Services Administration (PAGASA) is responsible. They gave it a local name: Yolanda. (To the dismay of feminist organisations, these destructive storms are inevitably given girls' names.) Moving at about 20mph Haiyan/Yolanda passed over the islands of Palau in Micronesia causing extensive damage but no deaths. Continuing to gain strength, its path now put the typhoon on track to hit the Philippines in the south of the country with the province of Leyte being most at risk. And the typhoon was becoming more violent by the minute. During 6 and 7 November, the Wednesday and Thursday, wind speeds within what was now classified as a super typhoon were reaching 145mph for periods of ten minutes and more. On the Thursday afternoon the Hong Kong Observatory was recording wind speeds of 180mph. The eye of the storm was heading for the Leyte port of Tacloban, a city of about 220,000. The authorities in the Philippines were bracing for a disaster.

But with the seas calm, barely a breeze rustling the palm fronds and local experience of storms and even typhoons creating little undue alarm, government agencies were finding it hard to persuade people to take shelter. It had begun to rain heavily on that Thursday afternoon. And up and down the coast, the fishermen were becoming nervous. The fish market was still bustling, but something was telling the fishermen this was no ordinary storm. There was little they could do but wait. While they waited the city authority prepared food packs and began evacuating people from coastal areas. The local health authority augmented their stocks of medicines: one of their number went unnoticed to check the number of body bags in the warehouse.

The people of Leyte had only to wait until Friday morning. While they sat at breakfast with their families, the storm arrived with terrifying speed and force. Windows and doors were blown open. Cups and plates were swept off tables. Outside, chairs and tables were being tossed aside. Sheets of rain blown horizontally were lashing against buildings that were still standing. Pick-up trucks were hurled into ugly heaps of rubber and metal. And then morning turned into night as the cloud and rain obliterated the sun and visibility dropped to less than 100 yards. Families who had taken shelter in churches gathered into terrified groups clinging to each other for comfort. Coconut palms were being torn out of the ground as the wind gusted at over 230mph. Then the mobile phones went dead. Families and friends, cut off physically, now had no way of staying in touch. Fear turned into desperation and terror.

And death came sure enough. Bodies – a few to begin with – began appearing amongst the debris of wrecked buildings. But the few became the many. Because what happened next had not been predicted or planned for. The city of Tacloban lies at the end of Cancabato Bay, a long bay that forms a perfect funnel. Had the eye of this super typhoon arrived just a few miles either to the north or the south, the worst might not have happened. But as it was, the typhoon caused a massive storm surge which sent a wall of water 20ft high into the bay and crashing over the city. People who had gathered in underground shelters were the first to die, drowned where they had been led to safety. Others were simply engulfed by the huge mass of water. Still others were picked up and hurled against buildings. Whole families died together in their fragile coastal homes. There were not enough body bags to go round. Within three terrible hours, more than 6,000 people had lost their lives. Today mass graves are marked by rows of simple white crosses. Those who survived had lost their livelihoods. An estimated 42 million coconut palms were destroyed and with them the livings of a million families. Farmers who could lay their hands on chainsaws began to clear the fallen trees before the rhinoceros beetle could settle in. Aid agencies were quick to respond bringing water and food. Tools and willing pairs of hands and advice on how to start afresh came too. But with so many coconut farmers already living below the poverty line, any rebuilding of the coconut farming community was not going to happen overnight.

Marcelina Calvez and her husband had been farming in Palompon, Leyte for more than thirty years. They have seven children and like many coconut farmers, they do not own their land. Even prior to Typhoon Haiyan, the half hectare of coconuts they were farming was not enough to meet their family's needs. 'After Haiyan, we lost our livelihood but we still had debts to pay,' said Marcelina. 'The hardest part was trying to earn money to feed my family.'

Four years on with memories of that terrible day when Yolanda destroyed lives and livelihoods still visible in the sad, empty eyes of so many plantation owners and workers, new dwarf palms are on the way to maturity which comes within four to six years. (The tall variety can take ten years to reach maturity.) Enrique, who survived the typhoon along with his 2-hectare plantation, says coconut farming is part of the Philippine culture, a way of life that has changed little since his grandfather worked the plantation. 'We will always grow coconuts here,' he says.

Philippine coconuts continue to find markets the world over. Exports of coconut products to America alone are worth some US $I billion per year. Procter and Gamble invested in the Philippines in the 1920s establishing their own direct supply of copra and coconut oil. Vita Coco, the leading brand of coconut water launched by New York friends Mike Kirban and Ira Liran in 2004, and valued by industry insiders at around US $1 billion, sources its coconut water in the Philippines. Europe has become the largest market for Philippine coconuts while total export sales in 2016 reached US $2 billion.

Activated coconut charcoal from the Philippines is used in the filters of gas masks in China; for extracting gold in the mining process in South Africa and Australia, and in gastro-intestinal drugs in Holland. Jars of Philippine coconut oil fill the shelves of health food shops from San Francisco to San Sebastian.

It is the Philippines and their neighbours in Indonesia who produce the bulk of the world's coconuts – Catholics and Muslims producing the nuts on which Hindus depend for their rights and rituals. True, the Hindus in India have their own supply from farmers in Kerala and Tamil Nadu where dense and numerous plantations make India the world's third largest supplier of coconuts, but in terms of cash-earning coconut products, the Philippines and Indonesia remain well out in front.

Indonesia currently claims the top spot as the world's number one producer. The country is such a huge sprawling archipelago that not even the Indonesians know how many islands there are. But they do know that the soil and climate of the large inhabited islands in the group provide ideal conditions for growing coconuts. Sulawesi, home to the singing Minahasans in the north; the Bugis and Makassarese in the south; the Toraja in the highlands who keep the bodies of the dead in their homes for months and sometimes years; transvestite shamans; animists, Buddhists, Christians and Confucians, manages to produce a full 20 per cent of Indonesia's coconut crop.

The Dutch established their source of copra here which proved essential to their margarine making. By the 1920s the Dutch East Indies, together with the Philippines, still at that time an American colony, were producing well over half the world's copra and the oil derived from it.

In 2014 Indonesia had a total of 3.6 million hectares of coconut plantations, more than 90 per cent of it farmed by smallholders working an average of just 1.5 hectares each. Copra and the oil derived from it still dominate the industry as they did a century ago, with scant research and development failing to encourage advances in production of the other products derived from the palm and its nuts. So farmers continue to produce copra by drying split halves of nuts in crude kilns – a process which takes about six hours.

The distribution of the copra from the farm to the oil mills involves several levels of traders, and that's where the farmers' profits all but disappear, just as they do in the Philippines. 'Small holders are not capturing a sufficient share of the profit in the supply chain,' Indonesia's Harvard-educated trade minister Thomas Lembong told a meeting of coconut producing countries.

The less energetic and less efficient farmers might be expected to sell their land to their more efficient neighbours. But land ownership in Sulawesi bestows dignity on the owner so everyone holds on to their land regardless of any financial incentives to do otherwise.

In Indonesia's Papua, the farmers in and around the village of Dabe are doing rather better. Dabe, a fishing village in the Sarmi Regency of northern Papua, has lost many of its fishermen to the coconut industry. Taught how to produce oil from copra by an aid team financed by New Zealand, both the men and women from Dabe and its neighbouring villages were soon producing enough copra to sustain two small oil factories employing one-time fishermen and their wives. 'We never did anything with the coconuts except eat them,' said one local fisherman-turned coconut farmer.

And where fishing had provided a meagre income, producing coconut oil within the community and without traders profiting from the distribution from farm to mill, has raised incomes considerably.

Several hundred miles to the west of Papua lies the small island of Kapoposang, a six-hour boat journey from Sulawesi. Here again the population had for decades made its living from fishing. But here they practised blast fishing – using explosives to stun or kill fish in shoals – and the explosives were destroying the habitat in which the fish lived. At least they were until a young Japanese woman visiting the area decided the local coconut oil was doing wonders for her skin. Ms Fujiwara contracted to buy 100 kilos of coconut oil every month for 'Love's Gallery' her café-cum-shop in Hyogo, on Japan's main island of Honshu. Within six months Ms Fujiwara had established a regular turnover of Kapoposang coconut oil, while the island's fishing community, buoyed by the new income from their coconut palms, had given up blast fishing and invested in new ecologically-sound equipment to cultivate lobsters.

On Indonesia's rather better-known island of Bali, the Day of Silence, a public holiday to mark the beginning of the new year, is just that, silent. Nobody works or travels anywhere; holiday makers are encouraged to stay in their hotels; aircraft are grounded; there is no entertainment, no shopping, and, for some, no eating. Instead there is meditating, contemplation and time for self-reflection.

On the day before Nyepi, as this silent day is known, things are a little different. Among the many high-spirited celebrations indulged in to mark the end the old year, young men thrash each other with flaming coconut husk to burn their demons and chase bad spirits away. During Ramadan on Java, fiery coconuts turn football into sixty minutes of health-and-safety-defying madness. A mass of husk is woven into a ball, soaked in kerosene and set alight. In bare feet two teams proceed to play a game of football with this uncompromising ball of fire. The game is popular in pesantren, Java's Islamic boarding schools. Low-cost dormitory living and a curriculum part general and part religious studies combine to provide an education where character development and vocational skills come high on the agenda. One headmaster told the *Jakarta Post* that the game 'increases confidence and bravery'. It was, he said, a way to praise God and that 'God gives us strength if we surrender to Him.'

So the players surrender and so far have all lived to play another day. But they take the precaution of covering their legs and feet in a combination of salt and non-flammable spices before taking to the field.

While the coconut is testing the bravery of young footballers on land, out in the waters of the Banda Sea it is giving succour to an octopus. Octopuses, blessed with decent sight and a well-developed brain, are accustomed to using foreign objects of all kinds as shelter. The hermit crab does the same mostly using discarded shells. What makes the veined octopus, *Amphioctopus margibatus* different is that it collects coconut shells for later use without gaining any protection while it is on the move. It puts two shell halves together to make a semi-permanent hideout.

Australian scientists have watched the octopus finding shell halves on the ocean floor, carrying them under their bodies and transporting them 60ft or more. The researchers say that while it is well known that octopuses are amongst the most intelligent of the invertebrates, these findings show just how capable these organisms are.

It was a British scientist exploring the oceans some 800 miles to the west of Indonesia, and a century and a half before the octopuses were first seen constructing their coconut shelters, who noted the existence of the coconut crab. Captain Robert Fitzroy, in command of HMS *Beagle* on her second voyage, had been given instructions by the Admiralty to investigate the formation of coral reefs, and to this end had set a course from Australia back to England via the Keeling Islands.

According to the diary of the young Cambridge-educated biologist Charles Darwin (Darwin was still only 27-years-old) the *Beagle* arrived at the small group of coral islands on 1 April 1836. The ship anchored in the channel that formed the entrance to the islands and was joined by an islander by the name of Liesk, an Englishman who had been first mate on a merchant ship that had visited previously and who now took pleasure in regaling his visitors with his observations of island life.

Chapter twenty of Darwin's *Voyage of the Beagle* records:

> The island has no domestic quadruped excepting the pig, and the main vegetable production is the cocoa-nut. The whole prosperity of the place depends on this tree; the only exports being oil from the nut, and the nuts themselves, which are taken to Singapore and Mauritius, where they are chiefly used when grated in making curries. On the cocoa-nut, also, the pigs, which are loaded with fat, almost entirely subsist, as do the ducks and the poultry. Even a huge land-crab is furnished by nature with the means to open and feed on this most useful production.

Darwin records his pleasure at sitting in the shade of a coconut tree and drinking 'the cool pleasant fluid of the cocoa-nut' and goes on to allude to what he describes as a monstrous crab which Mr Liesk had witnessed tearing away a nut's husk fibre by fibre and then hammering the nut with its powerful claws before extracting the white meat with its narrow pincers. The coconut crab was a good climber and strong enough to withstand inevitable falls from a considerable height.

All of which did not, 150 years later, entirely convince the UK's pre-eminent authority on the coconut, Hugh Harries, late of the Royal Botanic Gardens at Kew. While working in Papua New Guinea in 1983, Harries wrote a paper in which he suggested that Mr Liesk, noting his encounter with HMS *Beagle* to be taking place on 1 April, had played an April Fool on the young Darwin. Harries contends that Darwin's apparent observations are not his observations at all but those recounted to him by Mr Liesk who may, suggests Mr Harries, have been taking advantage of the date and of some company from home with whom to have some fun. No proof, says Harries, has been offered to confirm the crab's ability to crack a nut open and he is wary of film that claims to show the coconut crab climbing trees. 'Three questions remain,' wrote Harries,

> Did Mr Liesk really try to April Fool Charles Darwin? Did Darwin not know, or suspect, that the stories were nothing more than travellers' tales? Or did Darwin, in his turn and with tongue in cheek, publish the stories, knowing that many uncritical readers and fireside travellers would fail to see the significance of the date with which he opened his account?

3

CLEAN LIVING AND A TASTE OF PARADISE

By the beginning of the sixteenth century, the coconut had sustained hungry and thirsty mariners; been fashioned into ornaments that graced the palaces of bishops and the castles of kings; caused a mutiny at sea; featured in countless sacred texts; and been put to all sorts of uses in the countries of southern Asia and the South Seas where it flourished. In Europe a new-found hunger for the coconuts of the South Seas became insatiable as the Industrial Revolution in Britain gathered pace. And one man in particular was to build an empire based on what the coconut had to offer.

Creativity in British industry was as evident 250 years ago as it is today. The Industrial Revolution involved substituting the brute force of men, horses and bullocks with the power of machines driven by steam. One of the first industries to benefit from this mechanisation was the cotton industry. Richard Arkwright had developed spinning machines powered at first by horses and then by water. James Hargreaves came along with his invention of the cotton jenny and then Samuel Crompton combined the two into his spinning mule which gave the spinner much greater control over the weaving process. (Crompton subsidised his development of the mule by playing the violin in the pit of the Bolton theatre.) Steam-powered looms followed and Britain soon dominated the textile industry in Europe. Mechanisation and the mass production that came with it was changing Britain's fortunes, and the coconut was about to play a significant part in this transformation.

Not far from that theatre in Bolton where Crompton played his violin is Wood Street, where its Georgian houses provided an oasis of middle-class comfort in what was otherwise a drab and poverty-stricken town. At 16 Wood Street on 19 September 1851, Eliza Lever, the daughter of a cotton mill owner, gave birth to a son, her seventh child. The father, James Lever, owned a grocery shop and was delighted to have a son to continue the family business. They named their boy William.

William Lever entered the family business when he was 16. He was bright, hard-working and a voracious reader, forming a book club with a handful of school friends. The other boys in the school thought Lever and his friends were a bit odd. With other presents on the kitchen table on his 16th birthday he found a copy of Samuel Smiles' *Self Help*, the modest volume that espoused doggedness and conviction from the man described by George Bernard Shaw as 'that modern Plutarch'. The book was to prove a guiding influence in Lever's working life, and he bought copies for his friends and colleagues. Yet Lever was not stay-indoors bookish: he was get-up-and-go bookish. But not in his wildest dreams could he have foreseen that he would go on to found what became a colossal worldwide business, today worth nearly US $140 billion. But he did very quickly realise the potential of the coconut.

The Lever grocery business moved from retail to wholesale and young William was schooled in all aspects of the trade. He was still not yet 20 when he was given the job of collecting orders from the retail grocers in and around Bolton. Dressed in a suit, he did his rounds in a one-horse gig. But he was restless and began looking for ways to expand the business. The Industrial Revolution had spawned a huge increase in demand for soap. In the first half of the nineteenth century, production of soap in Britain trebled. Soap was not new. The Phoenicians used goats' tallow mixed with wood ash; the Romans washed clothes with tallow combined with urine. (Pots were left at street corners for people to add their own contributions and the urine left for several weeks to decompose and produce ammonia which proved to be an excellent cleaning agent.) The Celts mixed tallow with plant ash and called it *saipo*, and the British started making soap around AD 1200 in Bristol.

What was new in soapmaking was the gradual shift from tallow (animal fat) to saturated plant fats. Coconuts are high in saturated fats. Copra, the dried flesh or meat of the nut, produces the valuable fat-rich oil when crushed – the oil ideal for soapmaking. The venerable nut was about to underpin the development of a business making a variety of products that fast became household names. It was the 1880s and the economic conditions persuaded William Lever that the time was right to invest in soap manufacture. His father did not agree, at first believing they should stick to the grocery business which they knew and understood. But in the face of William's determination, his father's objections crumbled. William, with his brother Darcy, was given the money to take over a small soap works in Warrington. They took on works manager Percy Winser and soap boiler Edward Wainwright.

The new team at Warrington experimented with various ingredients to produce a better soap, and in the end settled on a blend of coconut oil (by far the largest ingredient) tallow, cotton oil and resin. The coconut oil came from crushing copra, the fleshy inner coating of the nut. Within a matter of months, the Lever brothers were turning out 20 tons a week of the new coconut soap. They branded the soap 'Sunlight'. And when the Warrington plant reached saturation point they found a site for a new factory between the River Mersey and the Birkenhead to Chester railway line. With the new Port Sunlight factory up and running, annual soap production was up to more than 15,000 tons. And the efficiency of the operation gave Lever much improved profit margins. This expansion meant Lever needed to increase his supply of coconuts. But demand for coconut oils and fats for the food industry had risen sharply and demand looked like outstripping supplies. So Lever proposed uniting the main players in the soap industry in order to exert leverage on the suppliers of the raw material, to centralise research and plough resources into the marketing of soaps in general. They called it the Soap Trust. (See p.5 of colour section.)

But the press did not like it. The Soap Trust, it raged, was counter to consumer interests. Northcliffe Newspapers led the attack with considerable success. Sales at Lever Bros were badly hit. Manufacturers outside the Trust were overwhelmed with orders as Northcliffe's *Daily Mail* laid into Lever with a host of accusations and innuendos.

The paper gloated over the losses the company was making as a result of their editorials. Lever consulted his lawyers and decided to sue Northcliffe for libel. Even before the case opened, Lord Northcliffe, realising his paper had overstepped the mark, offered Lever a public apology and a promise not to comment further on the Trust. Lever was having none of it. Barristers were briefed and the two sides went head to head at Liverpool Assizes before Mr Justice Lawrence.

The Northcliffe and *Daily Mail* case was weak. Their barrister, Rufus Isaacs, offered £10,000 to settle out of court. Once again Lever stood firm, and the country was treated to a piece of legal theatre in which counsel for the defence was bargaining in open court for a settlement. Isaacs' offer rose from £10,000 to £20,000 to £30,000 and finally £50,000. Lever accepted. Other papers admitted libel, and in all, Lever Bros received £91,000 in compensation (£10 million in today's money).

Able to concentrate again on expanding the business, William Lever set off by ship to find new sources for his soapmaking raw materials. In Ceylon (now Sri Lanka) and Samoa, where coconut palms were in abundance, Lever was alerted to the possibilities of producing his own copra and from it the oil he needed for his soap factory. Already in Ceylon and making a small fortune from its coconuts was another British entrepreneur called Henry Vavasseur. With his brother Josiah he had grown the family firm, exporting copra, oil and fibre, into an enterprise that dominated the island's coconut business. The Industrial Revolution in Britain had created an increasingly prosperous nation that could indulge itself in the occasional luxury beyond decent soap. Confectionery came high on the list and confectionery relied on desiccated coconut. But Ceylon's exported coconuts suffered a high percentage of spoilage which led Vavasseur to do some experiments on the copra – the meat of the coconut – with equipment used to dry tea leaves. With the copra dried and shredded, spoilage could be cut to a minimum. And as a considerable bonus, the desiccated coconut was much cheaper to ship. Commercial production of the desiccated coconut began in earnest and the brand was rapidly established in the UK and across much of Europe before entering the US market at the end of the 1890s. Ten years later, however, the US slapped heavy import tariffs on the Ceylonese desiccated coconut. Not to be outdone, Vavasseur turned his attention to the Philippines, still an American colony and exempt from the coconut tax as the colonial power sought to bolster the country's economy. He built new processing plants in the south of the country where the coconut plantations flourished – and where his company flourished too. The business diversified into tea, coffee and spices and continued trading until the end of the 1960s.

Meanwhile, Lever, having found his supplies of coconuts in Ceylon and Samoa, needed somewhere to set up a processing plant. He toured Australia and New Zealand, in part to develop markets for his soap but, more importantly, to look for a site to start processing the copra close to those new-found palm-growing regions of the South Pacific. At Balmain, then a working-class western suburb of Sydney across the water from Darling Harbour, Lever found the site he had been looking for. It was here he built a mill for crushing copra that he would ship from the islands of the South Seas in his own freighter, the SS *Upola*. And from here on the shores of Sydney harbour the barrels of oil would cross the world to the banks of the Mersey river. (See p.10 of colour section.)

By 1900 the Sydney mill was producing 92 tons of coconut oil a week. That same year, with a clear business logic but accompanied by plenty of grumblings from workers at home, Lever built a soap factory next to the mill. Lever was now making soap at both ends of the world. Sunlight and Lifebuoy became brand leaders. And the coconut had established itself at the heart of one of the great business empires of the twentieth century. Lever, however, was already looking beyond soap. 'I know of no field of tropical agriculture,' he wrote,

> that is so promising and I do not think in the whole world there is a promise of so lucrative an investment of time and money as in this industry. The world is only just awakening to the value of coconut oil in the manufacturing of artificial butter of the highest quality and of the by-product copra cake as a food for cattle.

As for artificial butter, the Dutch had stolen a march on Lever. But it was a Frenchman not a Dutchman who had set the ball rolling. In 1813 the French chemist Michel Eugene Chevreul discovered margaric acid, a combination of stearic and palmitic acids, and his 1823 treatise on animal fats became the basis for the modern knowledge of fats. Born in 1786 in Angers, he was educated in his native town before going, at the age of 17, to Paris, where he worked for the chemical manufacturer, Vauquelin. By the age of 20 he was contributing to scientific literature, and at 26 had attained the rank of professor at the Lycée Charlemagne. One of Chevreul's early pieces of research dealt with the manufacture of soap from spermaceti, the wax-like substance obtained from the head cavity of the sperm whale.

In 1813, Chevreul went on to make soap from lard and potash, from which he crystallised potassium stearate, a substance he called 'margaric acid'. Chevreul's 100th birthday in 1886 was celebrated with distinctions, honorary degrees and messages from every corner of the world, including one from Queen Victoria. His name joined those of seventy-two other French scientists engraved on the Eiffel Tower. But the chemist apparently disclaimed any particular merit save that of being 'the oldest among students in France'. He died in Paris two years and seven months later at the age of 102.

As has often been the case in the history of science it took a second chemist to realise the potential of another's work. But it was not until 1869 that the second chemist, in this case Mège-Mouriès, entered a competition staged by the Emperor of France himself. Napoleon III had offered a prize to anyone who could make a satisfactory alternative to butter, which would be suitable for use by the armed forces and the lower classes. The chemist won the competition with the product he called margarine, after its primary ingredient, 'margaric acid'. Mège-Mouriès patented the concept, expanded his initial manufacturing operation from France but had little commercial success. In 1871, just two years after the death of Chevreul, he sold his knowledge of the process to Jan and Henri Jurgens, brothers from a family of successful Dutch butter merchants, for 60,000 francs. Around the same time their rivals, the Van den Bergh family, also acquired a formula for margarine. High drama was about to unfold in the Lowlands.

But what started out as stiff and even aggressive competition between two family businesses operating in a small domestic market, soon turned to discussions about ways in which the two businesses could work together. The original ingredients of margarine were beef tallow and milk, but as demand increased, both companies began to turn to vegetable oils, especially coconut oil, to meet new production targets. A raw materials crisis in 1906 hit Jurgens and Van den Berghs hard, and after a series of pooling agreements, the two companies eventually merged to form a new organisation in November 1927 which they called Margarine Unie NV.

Lever was prompted by the Dutch move to use the fats he employed in soapmaking to make margarine himself. 'We drifted into the margarine business,' wrote Lever,

> because of its close connection with oils and fats for the soap kettle.* We drifted into West Africa, and the Congo, and the Solomon Islands to supply ourselves with oils and fats. Finding these oils and fats were even superior for margarine than for soap, we naturally diverted to and developed margarine manufacture.

It is hard to imagine Lever drifting into anything even if, by his own admission, the company did at one time show poor judgement around several rash acquisitions.

The Solomon Islands were providing the coconut oil when the impetus for beginning margarine production came with the outbreak of war in 1914. The expanded German navy posed a threat to supplies of butter from Denmark and margarine from Holland, and the British government approached Lever Bros about manufacturing margarine at home. The idea of going into the margarine business had been bouncing around the Lever boardroom for a couple of years prior to the outbreak of war, and a factory at Bromborough in the Wirral, on the south bank of the River Mersey, was hurriedly brought into production. The new plant was capable of turning out up to 3,000 tons of margarine a week. The coconut was already keeping people clean; now war was enlisting the coconut in efforts to keep people fed.

---

* Soap kettles were tall steel tanks with internal coiled tubing that circulated steam to melt the contents of the tank.

William Lever (Lord Leverhulme) William Strong 1918.

William Lever became a millionaire. He was elected to parliament in 1906 as the Liberal MP for the Wirral, where he had located his margarine factory. (The constituency has since been divided into Wirral West, which has the smallest electorate in England, and Wirral South. Both seats were held by Labour in the 2017 general election.) In his maiden speech to parliament Lever advocated a state-funded old age pension. He became a prominent Freemason, was knighted in 1911, and elevated to the peerage eleven years later. He died in 1925 at the age of 73. It was just four years later that Lever Bros merged with Margarine Unie of the Netherlands to form Unilever.

Margarine arrived in the United States in the 1870s, to the approbation of the poor, and to the universal horror of American dairy farmers. Within a decade there were thirty-seven companies in the United States enthusiastically manufacturing margarine. But they faced a continuing and fierce opposition from the butter makers, and in 1886 passionate lobbying from the dairy industry led to the federal Margarine Act, which slapped a restrictive tax on margarine and demanded that margarine manufacturers pay prohibitive licensing fees. Maine, Michigan, Minnesota, Pennsylvania, Wisconsin, and Ohio went a step further and banned margarine outright. (In Canada margarine was made illegal from 1886 to 1948.)

Margarine, its foes proclaimed, threatened the family farm, the American way of life, and the moral order. The rhetoric climbed to a new level. Impassioned speeches were made in defence of 'sweet and wholesome' butter. Governor Lucius Hubbard of Minnesota bemoaned the fact that 'the ingenuity of depraved human genius has culminated in the production of oleomargarine and its kindred abominations.' Senator Joseph Quarles of Wisconsin (the Dairy State) stoked the fiery debate by saying that butter should come from the dairy, not the slaughterhouse. 'I want butter that has the natural aroma of life and health. I decline to accept as a substitute caul fat,* matured under the chill of death, blended with vegetable oils and flavoured by chemical tricks'. Mis-information is nothing new: an advertisement in a 1911 edition of the *Chicago Tribune* showed arsenic, tin cans, and cats being thrown into the vat that mixed margarine.

* Caul fat is the fatty membrane that surrounds an animal's stomach.

Lever was not the first industrialist to make a fortune on the back of coconuts. When Queen Victoria married her Albert in Westminster Abbey on a chilly February day in 1840, millions of her loyal subjects lit celebratory candles in their front-room windows. The candles were made from a mixture of refined tallow and coconut oil.

The grand candles that lit the Abbey and the queen's palace at the end of the Mall were not, however, made from plant and animal fats but from beeswax. Beeswax had long been used for candlemaking but it was very expensive, and beeswax candles remained the preserve of the Church and the gentry. The white crystalline fat found in the head cavity of the sperm whale – the spermaceti – produced an excellent white and bright light but was even more expensive than beeswax. (And its name had many people convinced it was solidified sperm from the whale which did little for its popularity.) This left most people using the cheaper tallow candles that smoked and smelled. They were cheaper but not cheap. The government had long imposed a heavy tax on candles.

Two City of London livery companies, the Wax Chandlers and the Tallow Chandlers, presided over an inefficient industry badly in need of modernisation. That modernisation was initiated by business partners Benjamin Lancaster and William Wilson, a Scot who moved to London in 1812 when his father's ironworks collapsed in the financial chaos that had resulted from the Napoleonic Wars. Napoleon was withdrawing from the outskirts of Moscow as Wilson moved south.

In London, Lancaster and Wilson established a profitable trade importing goods from Moscow and St Petersburg as Russia rebuilt its economy. It was Lancaster, the younger man, who came up with the idea of making candles.

The two men were encouraged by the abolition of the candle tax and by the work of Michel Chevreul, whose experiments with fatty acids had already been put to use in the soapmaking business. The process known as saponification and used by soap makers was further refined by Wilson's son George for candle-making. The partners built their first candle factory at Vauxhall in south London, invested in a 1,000-acre coconut plantation in Ceylon, and built another factory upriver at Battersea to crush the coconut copra. They also invented Edward Price.

In the England of the 1830s there was an unwillingness amongst the middle classes to be associated with trade. And the use of smelly tallow from dead animals only made things worse: the whole business was perceived as an activity fit only for the lower working classes. So, rather than put their own names to their new enterprise, Wilson and Lancaster established Edward Price and Co. And by 1840 their candles combining refined tallow and coconut oil were ready for Victoria's wedding to Albert. Within ten years the company had expanded the business to include top-end candles – made mostly from beeswax – and were called on to supply candles for the funeral in 1852 of the Duke of Wellington. Six grand candlesticks mounted guard over his sarcophagus in St Paul's Cathedral. (Price's were later to provide the candles for the wedding of Princess Elizabeth and the funerals of Winston Churchill and Princess Diana.)

By 1880 Price's candles were part of the fabric of late nineteenth-century Britain, and by the end of the century Price's had expanded to dominate not just the domestic market but the market for candles worldwide. Lever Brothers, already well acquainted with the coconut, took over Price's candles in 1919 but not before George Wilson (William's son) had done the chemistry on glycerine for which he was awarded the Fellowship of the Royal Society. He had also formulated a new industrial lubricant, an oily liquid fat known as oleic acid which he separated from the coconut's fatty oil.

The newly mechanised wool and cotton manufacturers found this new lubricant superior to olive oil for keeping their looms running smoothly. Further refinements produced oil for rifles, bicycles, and a variety of engines. Rolls Royce selected Price's Motorine oil for their 1907 Silver Ghost, the first of their marques, and Price's oils were lubricating the British motorbikes that won at Le Mans in 1920. Britain had industrialised; the British people had grown more prosperous and the island nation that calls itself 'Great' was leading the way into the twentieth century. And at the heart of this economic expansion the coconut hung tall and proud.

In America, a revolution had seen off the British colonisers and yet it was an Englishman and an Irishman who were to build America's giant corporation based on soap – and coconuts. 'Cleanliness is indeed next to godliness,' asserted John Wesley, the founder of Methodism, in a sermon he called 'On Dress'. 'Indeed it is,' William Procter will have mused, rubbing his hands.

It took another two hundred years for *The Economist* newspaper to point out that the English language demonises dirt. It is packed with phrases such as 'to do the dirty', 'to dish the dirt' or 'dirty money' or 'dirty word'. In England, the paper noted, policemen are denounced as 'the filth'. All politicians seek to avoid 'washing their dirty laundry in public'. Those of humble origins were born 'dirt poor', and the wealthy are often 'filthy rich'. Getting rid of dirt, or merely its absence, by extension, is a good thing. 'A clean bill of health', 'a clean record', 'clean sweep', or 'good clean fun' evoke wholesome flawlessness, renewal or order. The act of washing, the newspaper continued, whether of a corpse in Jewish culture or of the hands and feet of the happy couple in a Hindi wedding ceremony, carries ritual symbolism in many cultures and faiths. Many religions link ablution to absolution.

William Procter, whose family had joined Wesley's Methodist fold, would have relished the notion of dirt being all-encompassing. Procter was by training another candlemaker who would make the natural progression to soap production. But this he did very far from home. Born in Herefordshire some years after Wilson in 1801, he was a true child of the Industrial Revolution.

He learnt the craft of candlemaking during his apprenticeship in the general store at home, before branching out on his own and setting up shop in London selling woollen goods. He had only been in the capital two days when his shop was set on fire and then ransacked by burglars. Some men would have headed home again with their tails between their legs. But Procter was made of sterner stuff. He was only 31 and already disenchanted with early Victorian Britain.

A friend of his father lent him £1,000, a hugely generous loan in those days, and with his wife Martha he left London for a new life in the American West. But disaster was to strike again. The couple had reached Cincinnati when Martha fell ill and was diagnosed with cholera. William nursed her but the disease had taken hold and Martha died soon after they arrived.

William decided against moving further west. He got a job in a bank while he grieved for his young wife. In time, his spirit and strength returned and he decided to put his knowledge of candlemaking to good use. He set up his own business on Main Street in the heart of Cincinnati and was soon doing a respectable trade, selling his candles locally and then expanding his markets to include stores in towns up and down the Ohio River.

Meanwhile an immigrant from Enniskillen in Northern Ireland, whose family had come to Cincinnati via Canada, had found himself a job in William Bell's soap and candle factory on Main Street just a block away. His name was James Gamble. The journey from Ireland with his family had been tough – forty-seven days to cross the Atlantic to New Brunswick, then down the coast to Philadelphia, three weeks in a cramped, bumpy wagon across to Pittsburgh and then five weeks drifting down the Ohio River.

Another immigrant, from County Tyrone in the south of Ireland, had established a tallow business in Cincinnati, a town so

William Procter (bearded) and James Gamble.

dominated by pig farmers it had earned the nickname *Porkopolis.* Alexander Norris had with him his wife and two daughters – Olivia and Elizabeth – and it was not long before James Gamble made the acquaintance of the eligible Elizabeth Norris. Their courtship was brief and the two married in the spring of 1833.

(The Irish community in Cincinnati was to grow over the years with a boost at the time of the potato famine in Ireland. By 1850 there were more than 30,000 Irish immigrants in the city. Even though these new immigrants were white, Christian and spoke English, they were unwanted and discriminated against by Cincinnati residents who had come earlier. Signs that read 'No Irish need apply' enforced discrimination.)

A year had passed since William Procter's wife Martha had died from cholera. The soap and candlemaking community in Cincinnati was a small one and many of them attended the same church, and it was not long before Elizabeth Norris was introducing the widowed Mr Procter to her sister Olivia. It was not love at first sight but the more the two saw of each other, the closer they became.

William eventually proposed, and when Olivia said 'yes' he made no attempt to hide his delight. They were to have ten children. The Norris sisters were now married to men in the same line of business. James had formed his own soapmaking business, and at times the brothers-in-law were in direct competition with each other. The girls' father, Alexander Norris, could see trouble ahead. He also saw the potential for combining James Gamble's and William Procter's individual strengths. It did not take much to persuade them to join forces. On a Tuesday at the end of October in 1837 Mr Norris bore witness to the formation of Procter and Gamble.

Ohio was home to America's pig farmers and Cincinnati was where the pigs were brought to slaughter, thus ensuring a ready supply of fat for the tallow users like Procter and Gamble. However, during the Civil War (140,000 Irish immigrants joined the Union army) which began in the second week of April in 1861, the demand for both candles and soap rose sharply, while supplies of tallow fat became scarce. Procter and Gamble were innovators and soon found new methods for making soap and candles that required less animal fat. They used coconut oil. They combined it with sodium hydroxide to form sodium cocoate which was adopted as the generic name for the mixture of fatty acid salts that result from the chemical reaction. It remains a critical ingredient in soap making today.

By the 1880s, Thomas Edison's electric light bulb was making the candle redundant – at least as a source of non-decorative light. Procter and Gamble decided it was time to concentrate on soap and to compete with the expensive European soaps that came hand-wrapped in pretty paper. When the civil war was over, American soap makers – Procter and Gamble included – returned to tallow as their main raw material. But unlike the European soaps which used vegetable oils, the soaps coming out of Cincinnati were coarse, heavy, smelly and discoloured.

So P&G turned once again to coconut oil. They added some palm oil, passed air through the mixture and produced a soap that not only looked and smelt pure but floated as well. They called it *Ivory*, and transformed their company from one that made soap and candles to one exclusively devoted to making soaps. The coconut had been essential in the foundation of Lever Bros and now in America it was underpinning the survival and growth of Procter and Gamble.

P&G, as Procter and Gamble came to be known (industry watchers refer to the company as 'The Kremlin' for its obsessive, some say paranoid, controlling management style), were not just innovators in the production of soaps, they were innovators in marketing too. Oxydol was one of P&G's first detergents. Its main rival was Rinso, a Lever Bros product, and Oxydol was losing out to the competition. But Rinso did not stay ahead for long.

P&G's innovative marketing men turned to sponsorship, investigating possible relationships with domestic serials on the radio. What they came up with was not only to catapult Oxydol into the top ranks of American detergents; it was to set a trend for broadcasters the world over. P&G's first sponsored radio show was a week-day serial called *Ma Perkins* about a salt-of-the-earth woman who owned and ran a lumber yard. The soap opera had been born. Each episode of the serial ran for fifteen minutes during which Oxydol got a mention not just once but on average twenty times. It started out on the local network and within four months was running nationally on NBC. Letters of complaint about the programme flooded into the P&G Cincinnati head office, but within a year, sales of Oxydol had doubled. And that's what mattered.

Radio drama sponsored by P&G heralded the arrival of the era of soap operas ('washboard weepies' to some). Debuting on WLW-Cincinnati Radio on 14 August 1933, *Ma Perkins* would grow to be the longest running radio soap opera. On 4 December 1933, *Ma Perkins* graduated to the NBC Red Network, where it was broadcast until 1949. In 1942, *Ma Perkins* was picked up by CBS Radio, when it was broadcast on both NBC and CBS simultaneously. Ma was the owner-operator of the lumber yard in the

Recording the *Ma Perkins* radio serial at NBC studios in the 1950s.

small southern town of Rushville, population 4,000. Storylines centred on her interactions with the local townsfolk as well as the ongoing dilemmas of her three children, Evey, Fay and John. The kindly, trusting widow Ma Perkins with her huge heart, and great love for humanity, was forever offering her homespun philosophy to any troubled soul in need of advice.

Actress Virginia Payne was a mere 23 years old when she took on the role of the matronly Ma Perkins. In the twenty-seven-year run of 7,065 episodes on the two networks, Virginia did not miss the taping of a single episode.

But the show was not without its critics. Many listeners found it irritating, but when Ma's son John was killed during the war, thousands of complainants wanting him back – from bereaved rather than irritated listeners – harangued the P&G head office. Marketing chiefs remained undaunted: having invented the soap opera P&G were not about to let broadcast sponsorship slip through their fingers. *The Guiding Light*, another radio soap, had its first episode on NBC in 1937, and then moved to television in 1952. It ran for a record seventy-two years.

As The World Turns, from the pen of *Guiding Light* creator Irna Phillips, the mother of broadcast soaps (see below) was P&G's last soap production for television. It entertained daytime audiences for fifty-four years and gave Julianne Moore her break in movies. (She had won a daytime TV Emmy for her role as Frannie Hughes, a psychologist who studied at Oxford University, and landed a role in *On the Darkside* when the soap closed.) With falling viewer numbers – down from 6 million a week in the 1990s to 2.5million in 2009 – the last episode was screened by CBS in 2010 after a run of 13,858 episodes.

There is no star on the Hollywood Walk of Fame for Irna Phillips. And that is extraordinary. (Donald Trump gets one for his role in the US version of The Apprentice. His star has been hacked to bits repeatedly, most recently in the summer of 2018 by a 24-year-old man who reportedly carried his pick-axe to the scene in a guitar case and told police he had been 'called' to action.)

Described in the *New York Times* as the 'Queen of Soapland', Irna Phillips created her first radio serial in 1930, and during a career that spanned more than forty years, wrote radio and television soaps that dominated daytime television in America – four were still on air when she died – and triggered a genre that would become an essential part of television programming and twentieth-century culture the world over.

Irna Phillips was born in 1901 in Chicago, one of ten children of German Jewish immigrants. Her father, a grocer, died when she was 8, and Irna grew into a quiet, retiring young woman happy with her books and her thoughts. By her teens she had decided she wanted to be an actress and enrolled in a drama course at Illinois University. But the acting opportunities failed to materialise so she enrolled in an education course and found work teaching drama and English. She had an affair with an English doctor and became pregnant. But the doctor abandoned her and the baby was stillborn leaving her sterile: events which not only affected her deeply but were to influence her script-writing. Desertion, divorce, illicit romance, strong independent women and illegitimate children were recurring themes in her dramas. She herself never married but adopted two children as a single mother. It was not an altogether successful family, with Irna unhappy with the adoptions and, she supposed, her children unhappy that she had adopted them.

Procter and Gamble (P&G) began sponsoring serials in 1933 and saw Phillips' storylines and characters as perfect material for the mainly female audiences they were trying to attract. She had identified the need for cliff hangers at the end of every episode, and introduced characters such as doctors, lawyers and teachers. And she delivered the first gay kiss on daytime television.

Her *Women in White* was the first serial set inside a major hospital. P&G's sponsorship of her *Guiding Light*, which ran first on NBC radio and then transferred to television with CBS, was the beginning of a decades-long relationship with the soap maker. The show ran for seventy-two years.

Her other huge hit *As the World Turns*, which premiered in 1956 also on CBS, clocked up 13,858 episodes over fifty-four years. For twenty of those years it held the top spot in television daytime ratings. The thirty-minute show was double the fifteen minutes given to serials at the time. Phillips saw the extended running time as an opportunity to better develop story lines and characters.

Procter and Gamble thought otherwise – at least to start with. So Irna, with the help of two colleagues, wrote and recorded a pilot thirty-minute edition of the show. P&G were quickly won over, and for the first twelve months the show diverted from the norm by concentrating on how the characters related to one another, and dwelling on the minute-by-minute emotions from which viewers gained their vicarious pleasure. Plot lines took second place.

However, it was a plot line, albeit not a very original one, that finally brought Irna's career to an end. It was in 1972, after forty years in the business, that she introduced a character she called Kim (played by Kathryn Hays) to *As the World Turns*. Kim was beautiful, single and longing for a baby. She had a one-night stand with her sister's husband and became pregnant. There was much of Irna in Kim: 'She is really me,' Irna told one interviewer. 'She is having a child out of wedlock. We are the same and she is going to have that child to prove she can do it alone.' Not only was she ahead of her time, sponsors Procter & Gamble questioned the morality of Kim getting the baby she wanted through adultery, and insisted that Irna change the story. But Irna was used to getting her own way: she was forceful and demanding at times, reducing cast members who did not meet her standards to tears. For her production company and for the sponsor, Irna Phillips, for all her talent, was becoming too difficult to work with. She was sacked, suffered a heart attack and died two days before Christmas in 1973. She was 72. She had pioneered a form of broadcast drama that commands huge and loyal audiences across cultures and across the social classes – and shows every sign of continuing to do so for generations to come.

A decade earlier, the British soap *Emmerdale* had won a £6 million P&G sponsorship deal for its makers Granada. The soap manufacturer was out to promote Daz. Surf, the competing Lever Faberge detergent, struck up a relationship with ATV's *Crossroads*. In front rooms across Britain a combination of soap, neighbourly drama and sex became required viewing.

While soaps won TV audiences in America and Britain, TV audiences in Andhra Pradesh, India's third largest market for soap, were being treated to some early reality shows. Unilever's Lux, the leading soap brand on the subcontinent, went on the hunt for a 'Lux Dreamgirl', in a sixteen-part reality caper designed to engage with its female target audience. The winner would be offered a lead in a locally made movie opposite one of the day's male heart-throbs. Fifty thousand aspiring young actresses applied in the first two weeks, and the show won huge audiences. Unilever in India saw awareness and sales of their beauty soap shoot up, and dream girl Aishwarya Gorak, a business studies graduate from the University of California at Los Angeles, had Bollywood at her feet.

Both Procter and Gamble and, on the other side of the Atlantic, Unilever continue to prosper as two of the world's leading consumer products companies, with both owing a lot to coconuts. And both radio and TV soaps continue to attract huge and loyal audiences. William Procter died in 1884 at the age of 83 and James Gamble was 88 when he died in his sleep on a summer's night in 1891. Lord Leverhulme died of pneumonia at his home in London. He was 73.

On the outskirts of Washington DC, almost exactly 500 miles due east of Cincinnati, is the community of McLean, an upmarket suburb of the capital and home to politicians, diplomats and sundry Washington movers and shakers. Gore Vidal, Ted Kennedy, Colin Powell, Dick Cheyne and the Saudi ambassador have lived here. CIA headquarters at Langley is just 1½ miles away.

It is also the home of a company that makes an awful lot of chocolate. This is where Mars Inc. runs its international candy business from a nondescript, distinctly non-corporate, two-storey building with a staff of less than 100. One look at its corporate headquarters makes it hard to believe that Mars is the third richest private company in the US. (When the head of Nestlé arrived

Frank Mars with his mother Alva *c.* 1886.

at the building for a formal visit, he thought he was in the wrong place.) The executive offices are on the second floor. Victoria Mars, unmarried, worth an estimated US $6 billion and the great-granddaughter of the company's founder Frank Mars, was the last of his direct descendants to hold high office.

Great-grandfather Frank was born in Hancock, Minnesota in 1882. As a child he developed polio which prevented him from walking to school. His mother Elva turned their kitchen into a classroom and when the school work was done taught him how to make chocolate. At the beginning of the twentieth century no one worried much about a balanced diet; cholesterol was little understood (although scientists were hinting that cholesterol was related to atherosclerosis around 1910) and fatty acids had yet to be put under the microscope. What's more, there was just enough sugar to go round. So there was little to inhibit the entrepreneurial spirit of Frank and his second wife Ethel, from establishing a cottage industry making buttercream candy in the kitchen of their new home in Tacoma, a port city on Puget Sound in the shadow of Mount Rainier in Washington State. Frank made the candy, and Ethel sold it to local retailers.

Frank's son Forrest, from his first marriage to another Ethel (Ethel Kissack) was just 6 when his parents divorced. Forrest proved an able and ambitious young man. He went to Yale and Harvard Business School before joining his father and stepmother in what had finally become an expanding chocolate business. (The couple's earlier efforts at creating a candy business had failed miserably.) Together the three of them developed a chocolate bar they called Milky Way. It was a huge and immediate success. (Ethel continued to train race horses, and when she and Frank invested in a 3,000-acre farm in Tennessee and moved the horses there, they called it Milky Way Farms. In 1936 the Milky Way stables topped the horse-race winnings league in the United States.)

But father and son squabbled, and Forrest left for England in 1932 with modest financial backing from his parents and the Milky Way formula – and the rights to market it in Europe – in his pocket. Across the River Thames from the queen's castle at Windsor, he found premises in Slough, an industrial town given lifelong infamy by her majesty's poet laureate John Betjeman:

> Come friendly bombs and fall on Slough!
> It isn't fit for humans now.

Unperturbed, Mars settled in Slough, made lots of chocolate, fiddled with the Milky Way recipe and renamed his refined product the Mars bar. He began by selling his new chocolate bars off a tray in the local market. He had a staff of four and lived in a one-bedroom flat at the back of the works. Modest beginnings would quickly develop into a very substantial business, thrusting Mars head-to-head with a second American chocolate maker, Hershey (the two now share some 75 per cent of the sweets and chocolate business in the US).

Staff at the expanding Slough factory were bound by the five principles which underpin the Mars business ethic: quality, responsibility, mutuality, efficiency and freedom. Everyone was an associate and on first name terms with everyone else – even if some on the shop floor found it difficult greeting the boss by his first name. The offices were open plan. The managing director had no office, just a desk like all the managers working under him. Every member of staff, senior managers included, clocked in, and everyone was responsible for ensuring that he or she was on station in their white coats six minutes before their shift started. Office staff were subject to the same discipline. Punctuality was paramount. One former staffer recalls being overtaken on the stairs by the managing director, conscious that with fines for latecomers based on their salaries, he had more to lose than the rest of them. Any other business would celebrate the success Mars was having in Slough by rewarding the boss with a little luxury. Not so Mars Inc. Forrest Mars had no chauffeur and no company car. Only salesmen had company cars. There was a staff car park but no spaces reserved for senior management – they had to find a space like everyone else. Forrest would arrive unannounced. He was a big man, almost entirely bald, an Episcopalian, twice married, with a tendency to be blunt and on occasions even rude. He would settle himself on the corner of someone's desk and ask no one in particular how they had been spending the company's money. Not how they had made money but how they spent it.

Spending it had its limitations. With limited scope for reinventing a bar of chocolate, the rivalry between Mars and its competitors became intense. Which explains how Forrest Mars Sr came to emulate, if not copy, a bar produced by one of the smaller players, Peter Paul Candies. Peter Paul Halajian was an Armenian immigrant. With five of his fellow countrymen, he established a chocolate manufacturing business in New Haven, Connecticut in 1919. Their first product was a chocolate-covered coconut bar with nuts and fruit. Taking out the fruit and the nuts and refining the chocolate coating, they relaunched the bar a couple of years later calling it *Mounds*. The new bar flew off the shelves, defied the recession and twenty years later became a favourite with American soldiers serving in the Second World War. The US Department of War bought 5 million *Mounds* every month during the war ensuring that every soldier had a coconut bar in his rations.

(War was also the trigger for one particular Mars success. Forrest Sr had travelled to the south of Spain during the civil war where he met soldiers feeding off small pellets of chocolate in a sugary shell – a shell that prevented the chocolate from melting. Mars persuaded Bruce Murrie, the son of Hershey's president, to join him in a one-off venture and together they produced M&Ms (Mars and Murrie) the sugar-coated chocolate drops that roll off the Mars production lines in their multi-coloured millions every hour.)

Meanwhile, the success of *Mounds* had not escaped the attention of Mr Mars and in 1951 the company began production of its own version of the chocolate coconut bar in Britain and Canada. They called it the *Bounty* bar. With Peter Paul Candies yet to break into either of those two markets, *Bounty* became a major brand for Mars. The 'taste of paradise' TV adverts promising that one bite of a *Bounty* would lead to palm-sheltered sexual liaisons on tropical islands were an instant hit with television audiences unused to alluring flashes of female flesh.

Today *Bounty* bars are made in their millions at the Mars facility at Veghel in the Netherlands and sold in wrappers whose design has changed little in sixty years – blue wrappers for the milk chocolate variety and red for the plain dark chocolate covering. And it is not just the wrappers that have not changed; the design of the bar itself has not changed either.

In 2003 Mars Inc. decided to trademark the shape. Not so fast, said EU legislators. While Rome burned, Brussels pondered long and hard over the chevrons in the chocolate covering of the *Bounty* bar. The European Court of First Instance in Luxembourg declared:

> The allegedly distinctive characteristics, namely the rounded ends of the bar and the three arrows or chevrons on top of it, cannot be sufficiently distinguished from other shapes commonly used for chocolate bars.

The verdict was a victory for Ludwig Schokolade, a German chocolate maker who had been making chocolate-covered coconut bars for British supermarkets since 1990. The company challenged a decision taken by the EU's trademark office in 2003 to approve Mars' application to register the *Bounty*'s shape as a trademark across Europe. The trademark office backed the German firm by declaring the *Bounty* 'shape' trademark invalid, on the grounds that it was not distinctive enough because the shape 'does not depart significantly from the norms and customs of the relevant sector'.

Mars then turned to the Court of First Instance, which acknowledged that a shape could be trademarked if it had acquired 'distinctive character following the use made of it'. But judges in the European Court, while accepting the principle set down by the Court of First Instance, decided it did not apply in the case of the *Bounty* bar and refused Mars permission to register the shape of the bar as a trademark.

No matter. Mars Inc. continues to churn out millions of tons of chocolate including the *Bounty* bar. In the US it is the number one chocolate maker by sales, and remains the leader by market share worldwide. The diversified company – it produces pet foods and some grocery products as well as chocolate – is still privately owned by the very private Mars family.

(So private is Mars Inc. that a caller in the US asking for the name of the company president was advised that that kind of information was not available, and an enquiry to company media representatives in London about *Bounty* bar production in Europe met with the same response. No one is sure exactly how old Victoria Mars is, and few would dare ask.) Forrest Mars Sr died in 1999 at the age of 95, handing the company over to his son Forrest Jr who died seventeen years later. While senior executives on today's Mars board may not be direct descendants of Frank Mars, family members still hold a controlling interest in the business.

The technology involved in making chocolate, though complex and well refined, is nothing compared with the technology that will be required to produce electricity in the second half of the twenty-first century. In the south of France, in the commune of Saint-Paul-Les-Dur just north-east of Aix-en-Provence, that technology is feeding a project that could change the way we live. Thirty-five countries including the United States, Germany, France, Russia, China, Japan, India and the UK are working together to explore a new means of powering our future.

In a highly ambitious project, ITER, the International Thermonuclear Experimental Reactor (successor to the Joint European Torus pilot project at Culham in Oxfordshire) will test the feasibility of producing the form of energy created in the heart of the sun where hydrogen nuclei collide releasing energy in colossal amounts. Nuclear fusion, as opposed to nuclear fission, the current form of nuclear energy, involves creating an environment where hydrogen nuclei can collide in a vacuum at very high temperatures. If it can be made to work, nuclear fusion promises a cheap, safe and clean form of energy. But there is a big 'if'. In order to create the necessary vacuum, ITER requires very high pumping speeds and so uses cryopumps that work by trapping gases on a cold surface. The cooled surface is partly covered with a porous material that can adsorb the gases in the same way that poisonous gases are trapped in the filters of gas masks.

In ITER's case, tests carried out by the Karlsruhe Institute of Technology in Germany on many different adsorbing materials showed that activated charcoal made from a particular vintage of coconuts from a plantation in Indonesia gave the best results. The nature and size of the pores on the surface of the charcoal proved to be super-efficient in capturing the unwanted helium. ITER bought up all the supplies available and, fifteen years on, there is no sign of degradation in the charcoal's performance. Robert Pearce, the British engineer who leads the vacuum team at ITER, expects the same charcoal to be working efficiently after another thirty years. However, the project has now moved on from its original Indonesian coconuts and now holds a stock of 400kg of contemporary coconut charcoal in the basement of its headquarters.

Pearce, who moved from Culham to France, points out that coconut charcoal is a filter suited to all kinds of liquids and gases – including the water he drinks. In his rural part of France there is no connection to a piped water supply so his water comes directly from the canal. He then filters it through his personal supply of activated coconut charcoal. He also has a small supply of whole coconuts which have proved essential to the smooth running of the ITER enterprise. His cryostat workshop – a 500sq. metre giant thermos – was built and pre-assembled in fifty-four units by ITER's Indian partner in Gujarat. The departure by low-loader of each unit has been accompanied by traditional Hindu ceremonies of coconut smashing to ensure the cargo's safe journey. The ritual concludes when coconuts are placed under the lorry's wheels as it drives out of the factory gates. By the same token, when each stage of the assembly is near completion on site in the south of France – a process that remains the responsibility of the Indian partner – more coconuts are smashed to ensure the satisfactory operation of the machine. If nuclear fusion becomes a reality, coconuts will be at the heart – technically and spiritually – of power production for decades to come.

Fusion or no fusion, the coconut is already at the forefront of technology that brings clean power onto the world's roads, and clean air into people's cars. The number 11 bus route in Shanghai does a loop starting and finishing at Laoximen in the old quarter of the city. Route 26 connects Hongqiao with Gao'en Road via Xinbeimen, Middle Jinling Road, ShaanXi Road and Changshou Road, running from 5.30 a.m. in the morning till 10.45 p.m. at night. The two lines, and a rapidly increasing number of other city routes, operate electric buses that use supercapacitors jam-packed with coconut charcoal. The buses charge their capacitors at bus stops with an arm on the bus roof that rises to connect with the overhead supply. And unlike charging a conventional battery which takes time, the supercapacitor is fully charged by the time passengers have climbed off and on. The city, which sprawls on both sides of the Huangpu River, has a population of 24 million served by no less than 1,000 bus routes. Compared with public transport in London and New York, fares on Shanghai's buses are a bargain. Add to that the fact that an ever-increasing number of the city's buses are pollution free, and you get a cheap and clean form of inner-city transport which leads the world.

'Clean' though some of China's buses might be, other factors that determine the quality of the air in the country's larger cities continue to create semi-permanent smog or, at best, levels of pollution that create serious health risks. Enter, once again, the coconut. China's hotels, fearing air pollution will prove to be bad for business, provide gas masks (with coconut charcoal filters) as one of the standard room amenities. The glitzy Fairmont Hotel in Beijing's central business district presents their masks in crimson velvet bags emblazoned with the hotel's crest.

Smokers in China, and increasingly in Japan, Russia and south-east Asia have taken to smoking filter-tips containing the now ubiquitous coconut charcoal. The charcoal removes some of

A bridal couple in Beijing, Zhang Xinyu and her groom Bal BeiBei wear charcoal filter gas masks as protection against the city's pollution. (Rex Features)

the toxicants, which in turn reduces the damage to the smoker's mouth and lungs. The cigarette manufacturers promote the filter-tips as flavour enhancers. By extracting some of the cigarette's toxicants their customers get a degree of protection, live a little longer – and buy more cigarettes.

In the United States, healthy drinking water is being delivered at a cost. The high levels of chlorine needed to keep the water safe are proving unpopular with householders who are filtering their tap water at home. Brita is one filter manufacture that boasts its use of coconut charcoal.

Not surprisingly, filtering with coconut charcoal has become big business. Coconut charcoal is a traded commodity, and while prices fluctuate according to the supply of nuts – a supply influenced mostly by climatic conditions – recent years have seen a metric ton reach a premium of US $600. The Swedish company

Jacobi Carbons is the world's largest manufacturer of coconut shell activated carbon. A wholly owned subsidiary of the Japanese chemicals giant Osaka Gas Chemicals, Jacobi's processing plants in the Indian subcontinent and across south-east Asia consume more than 200,000MT of coconut charcoal per year, requiring more than 3.2 billion coconuts to produce a more modest 70,000MT of activated carbon. Forty trucks loaded to the gunwales deliver basic coconut charcoal to the five processing plants every day.

However, a gram or two is all it needs to keep a cat smelling sweet. Their grooming products don't yet contain coconut oil nor does the average tin of cat food contain desiccated coconut. And when it comes to a saucer of milk, cats seem perfectly content with a helping of cow's milk. But for those less well-trained cats that use a litter for their convenience – not to mention the convenience of their owners – coconut charcoal in the litter adsorbs the odour of the gases emanating from the cat poo.

4

THE COCONUT GOES TO WAR

The car took a wrong turn and dragged Europe into a terrible, devastating war. Earlier in the day a bomb had been thrown at the royal vehicle injuring an army officer but failing to harm either of the car's occupants. When it was time to return home, security advised taking an alternative route back to the railway station. But there was a breakdown in communications and no one told the car's driver. So he followed the original route until an officer travelling with them put him right. He stopped the car, began turning it around and just as the car was briefly motionless, was confronted by a member of the activist cell that had earlier thrown the bomb. His name was Gavrilo Princip, a student activist just 19 years old and suffering from tuberculosis. He drew a gun and fired twice at close range killing both passengers – Archduke Franz Ferdinand and his wife Sofie. It was 28 June 1914 – their wedding anniversary.

The assassination on that street in Sarajevo in the summer of 1914 prompted the chain of events that would lead to the First World War. While the protagonists of the war – Serbia, Germany, France, Russia, Britain, Belgium and Austria-Hungary – were preparing their battle lines, a factory in Stockerau, just 30km north-west of Vienna from where the Archduke had begun his fateful journey, was going about its business turning coconut charcoal into a super adsorption product they called *Eponit.* The management and workforce of the Fanto-Werke factory could not in their wildest dreams have imagined the shooting of their Archduke and his wife would turn the development of coconut charcoal into one of the defining factors of modern warfare.

From the very beginning of the Great War, there was the ever-present risk that Germany would resort to chemical weapons, and this risk soon developed into a permanent threat for the foot soldiers on the front line across Europe. That threat became a reality when the first major gas attack was launched at the end of January in 1915. Germany's Ninth Army released 18,000 gas shells on the Russian lines at Bolimov in what is now Poland.

The German commander, General Max Hoffman, watched the operation from the tower of a church that overlooked the battlefield. He found it hard to believe what he was seeing. The gas, a form of tear gas, appeared to have little effect. The German scientists who had created the gas had failed to investigate how it reacted in the bitter cold of winter. In fact the gas froze, the Russians appeared bemused and the gas attack proved a miserable failure. From his lookout, General Hoffman watched in disbelief, humiliated and very angry.

Shamed but undaunted, the scientists, headed by the Jewish chemist Dr Fritz Haber, who had led the way in synthesising ammonia (for which he would be awarded the Nobel prize for Chemistry at the war's end) went back to their laboratories. Haber with his shaven head, neat moustache, pince-nez and carefully buttoned white lab coat drove his team hard and within a couple

A Swedish postage stamp issued in 1978 commemorating Dr Fritz Haber, the German chemist who won the 1918 Nobel Prize for chemistry for his industrial production of ammonia. During the First World War, he was in charge of the development and production of Germany's poisonous gases.

of months, had refined his chlorine gases and the canisters that would deliver them. The German High Command was delighted. Haber's wife Clara was appalled. She too was a scientist and was idealistically opposed to science being used to develop such horrific weapons. She implored her husband to disband his development work, and when he refused and proceeded to come up with still more lethal gases, she shot herself through the heart with her husband's revolver. For Haber, the survival of the Fatherland was more important than the death of his wife and he took himself off to see his latest chemical weapons in action. (His lengthy and highly complimentary biography on the Nobel Prize website manages to reduce his work on the poisonous gases which killed tens of thousands of allied soldiers to 'he organised gas attacks and defences against them.' His son by his marriage to Clara followed his mother by committing suicide.)

It was a very different story when the Germans dropped Haber's new pressurised gas cylinders on French Algerian troops at the beginning of the second battle for Ypres in 1915. The attack was launched at sunrise in late April. As the 5,700 cylinders exploded, releasing hundreds of tons of chlorine, a yellow-green cloud of gas drifted across the allied trenches. The French were unprepared and unprotected. 5,000 died from asphyxiation within ten minutes of inhaling the gas; others were temporarily blinded and having difficulty with breathing. In the confusion, advancing German troops equipped with rudimentary gas masks took 2,000 prisoners. A Canadian medical officer, who was also a chemist, quickly identified the gas as chlorine and recommended that the troops urinate on a cloth and hold it over their mouth and nose. Up till now, the coconut was still in the wings. But its time would come.

The attack caused outrage: '*DEVILRY, THY NAME IS GERMANY*,' howled the *Daily Mirror*. The commander of the British Expeditionary Force, Sir John French, described the use of gas as 'a cynical and barbarous disregard of the well-known usages of civilised war'. But within four months Sir John was changing his tune: 'Owing to repeated use by the enemy of asphyxiating gases in their attacks on our positions, I have been compelled to resort to similar methods,' he said. General Karl von Einem, who commanded Germany's Third Army in France wrote: 'War has nothing to do with chivalry anymore. The higher civilisation rises, the viler man becomes.'

The threat of gas did as much damage psychologically to soldiers on the front line as it did physically. It created a sense of terror which, for many men, was greater than the terror of bullets and bayonets. Professor Edgar Jones of the King's Centre for Military Health Research in London identified many cases where the fear of gas had spread from one platoon to another with devastating effect. Adolf Hitler, as a young corporal, was so terrified of being gassed he left the army for politics. (See p.8 of colour section.)

'In a war of attrition,' notes Professor Jones, 'morale is critical and this (the use of poisonous gas) was an attempt to undermine morale.' John Singer Sargent's 1918 painting which depicts blinded soldiers with bandages covering their eyes, walking in line, one hand on the soldier in front, became known simply as *Gassed.* The painting was a departure from Sargent's portraiture and pastoral scenes. Commissioned by the British War Memorials Committee, Sargent travelled to the front line spending time with the American expeditionary force near Ypres. He did not complete the picture until March of 1919 when the war had ended. He collected his £600 fee but the picture received a mixed reception. It is now part of the collection at the Imperial War Museum. The young Wilfred Owen's First World War poem *Dulce et Decorum Est,* written between October 1917 and March 1918, is concerned with the same subject describing, as it does movingly, the effects of the green clouds of chlorine gas that created the terror in the troops:

Bent double, like old beggars under sacks
Knock-kneed, coughing like hags, we cursed through sludge
Till on the haunting flares we turned our backs
And towards our distant rest began to trudge.
Men marched asleep. Many had lost their boots
But limped on, blood-shod. All went lame; all blind;
Drunk with fatigue; deaf even to the hoots
Of tired, outstripped Five-Nines that dropped behind.

Gas! Gas! Quick boys! – An ecstasy of fumbling,
Fitting the clumsy helmets just in time;
But someone still was yelling out and stumbling,
And flound'ring like a man in fire or lime...
Dim, through the misty panes and thick green light,
As under a green sea, I saw him drowning.

In all my dreams, before my helpless sight,
He plunges at me, guttering, choking, drowning.

If in some smothering dreams you too could pace
Behind the wagon that we flung him in,
And watch the white eyes writhing in his face,
His hanging face, like a devil's sick of sin;
If you could hear, at every jolt, the blood
Come gargling from the froth-corrupted lungs,
Obscene as cancer, bitter as the cud of vile, incurable sores on innocent tongues.
My friend, you would not tell with such high zest
To children ardent for some desperate glory,
The old Lie; *Dulce et Decorum est*
Pro patria mori.

The first substance designed to offer protection against chlorine and phosgene gases was activated carbon from the charcoal of red cedar. But this did not work against the gases most likely to be deployed. Almonds, Arabian acorns, grape seeds, Brazil nuts, Chinese velvet beans, coffee grounds and peanuts were all reduced to carbon, tested, but found wanting. Enter the coconut. Hindu documents dating back to 450 BC refer to coconut charcoal filters being used as water purifiers. In many parts of the developing world south of the equator the woody shell is burned as fuel. And while the charcoal created was of little interest to the people of the South Seas, it did interest scientists in Europe and America. First to identify the adsorption properties of powdered charcoal was John Hunter, working at Queen's College in Belfast in the 1870s. He discovered that powdered coconut charcoal presented extraordinary powers of gaseous adsorption. By the turn of the century Raphael Ostrejko, a chemist born in Latvia of Polish parents, was working on a process that would considerably increase the charcoal's adsorption powers. Ostrejko passed steam at high temperatures through the powdered charcoal and found the adsorption powers of the charcoal were increased by 100 per cent.

A factory in Stockerau in lower Austria went into production calling their activated charcoal *Eponit.* Although the tiny pores on the surface of activated charcoal are less than 4 nanometres in diameter, they greatly increase the surface area of the powder – four capsules of activated coconut charcoal would cover a football pitch. The pores trap molecules of a wide range of toxins, including chlorine and 2-chloroethyl sulphide, the gas commonly known as mustard gas. This property made coconut charcoal attractive to chemists looking for the most effective ways of filtering poisonous gases.

'We have been using activated carbon to remove toxic gases for a century or more,' notes Gregory Peterson, leader of today's gas mask filtration research group at the Edgewood Chemical Biological Centre in Maryland. 'Coconut charcoal exhibited the additional qualities of being chemically stable and therefore remaining active for long periods; it was resistant to abrasion and offered protection against a wide variety of gases.'

But few ever thought that poisonous gases would be used as a weapon of war. So following the chlorine gas attacks at Ypres, scientists and engineers in the UK and in the US had to go into overdrive in their search for an effective mask. While a number of researchers claim to have been the first to link the activated coconut charcoal with wartime gas attacks, it seems likely that Nikolai Zelinski, a senior organic chemist at the university in Moscow, prompted by the gas attack on Russian troops at Bolimov, was the first to stuff the charcoal into the filters of gas masks. Defence establishments in Europe and America were quick to follow his lead.

In the United States the search for used coconuts began in earnest with the gas defence division of the Chemical Warfare Services writing an open letter to the Franklin Baker Coconut Company. 'We are finding it difficult to secure a sufficient quantity of coconut shells to meet our requirements,' the letter began. It explained that the 'best material that has been found for gas masks' was likely to run short if sufficient coconuts could no longer be imported.

The letter was incorporated in an advertisement in women's magazines encouraging housewives to use recipes that included coconut, and then make the shells available for collection by government agencies. Another newspaper advertisement headed 'Fighting German Gas-Shells with Coconut-Shells' extolled the culinary qualities of the nut and reminded Americans that by giving coconut 'a regular and frequent place on your weekly menu, you are also helping your government.'

The advertisements helped, and tons of coconut shells were delivered to government collecting stations and sent on to the Edgewood Chemical Biological Centre at the US Army's Aberdeen proving ground in Maryland. But this still was not enough, and a charcoal plant was established in the Philippines (still an American colony at the time) with agents scurrying across south-east Asia, buying up huge quantities of coconut shells. At Edgewood 25,000 small, self-contained box respirators were produced in 1917. Each consisted of a mouthpiece connected to a metal box filter containing the coconut charcoal and soda lime. During the following year Edgewood produced 3 million of an improved version. Two million were shipped to Europe. The Hero Manufacturing Company in Philadelphia, Pennsylvania was one of several firms charged with adding to the supply of masks for the US Expeditionary Force in Europe. Its rate of gas mask production rose to 2,430 a day.

A similar plea for coconut shells was issued in Britain by the National Salvage Council after the large quantities of coconuts imported from Ceylon still failed to meet the demand from mask manufacturers. Thousands of women toiled long hours in factories large and small that had turned from producing peacetime goods to making gas masks. At Melksham in Wiltshire, the Avon Rubber Company which had produced pneumatic bicycle tyres, tennis balls and tyres for Rolls Royce cars, switched to manufacturing gas masks. The Avon ladies worked around the

School children in Liverpool take part in a gas attack exercise during the Second World War.

clock producing some 20 million masks by the end of 1939. Up and down the country, civil defence workers, air raid precaution officers and St John Ambulance volunteers were encouraging the population to ready themselves for gas attacks. Audiences in village halls and town halls never ceased to be surprised that the key element in the masks they were being shown was coconut.

By the end of 1939, 36 million masks had been distributed in Britain. The Government believed that war would be certain to mean gas attacks from the very start of hostilities. While the gas attacks never materialised, the fear engendered by the possibility that every air raid could be the one to bring blinding, choking, asphyxiating gases meant the masks provided comfort and vital psychological assurance for every man, woman and child. Without the masks, the morale of the civilian population would have been tested beyond endurance.

While the coconut offered protection to millions of service personnel and civilians as war once again enveloped Europe, the bombing by the Japanese of Pearl Harbor in 1941, and the subsequent United States entry into the Second World War saw the coconut keeping bad company in the chemistry department at Harvard University. Conducting his experiments in secret in the university's Gill laboratory, Louis Fieser, an organic chemist in his forties who had moved to Harvard from the University of Oxford, was working for the US Defence Department on incendiary devices – a top secret project operating under the guise of 'Anonymous Research project No 4'. It was on Valentine's Day in 1942 that Fieser, whose justifiable claim to fame had been the synthetic production of cortisone, hauled a 70lb napalm bomb to the centre of a lagoon he had constructed behind the library of the university's business school. Fire trucks from the city of Cambridge took up their positions, the firemen unsure of what they were about to witness. No one on the nearby tennis courts seemed to take much notice. Fieser ran a detonator cable from his 'bomb' in the lagoon to dry land. With everyone at a safe distance he pulled the switch. The billow of fire which rose over the ground reached temperatures of more than 2,000°F as lumps of fiery napalm splashed into the lagoon. One of Fieser's team described a smell like garlic mixed with the sickly aroma of gasoline.

The test was deemed a success. To gasoline Fieser had added a brown dry powder consisting of two parts of coconut oil acid, one part of naphthenic acid and one part of oleic acid. It had all been quite simple. 'You just take gasoline, sprinkle in some powder and stir,' he somewhat flippantly told Harvard's *Crimson* newspaper in a 1973 interview. The US Army's Chemical Warfare Service took over the testing, and found Fieser's napalm highly satisfactory.

Professor Louis Fieser.

Within days, the Dow Chemical Corporation was commissioned to begin production of napalm on a commercial scale.

Further testing and research into how best to deliver this very effective napalm was moved to the US Army's high security Dugway Proving Ground in the Utah desert some 90 miles from Salt Lake City. The burning gasoline would stick to most surfaces including human skin. The question was in what form would it stick to the greatest number of surfaces and do the most damage. A hectic but very carefully planned programme of tests took place between May and September of 1943. First, two sets of buildings were constructed to replicate targets in Japan and Germany. To best judge the effectiveness of the napalm bombs that were being developed, these buildings had to be detailed reproductions of middle-class housing in Tokyo and similar quality housing in a typical German city. The Czech architect Antonin Raymond, who had worked in Japan before settling in the US, led the design and construction of the Japanese homes. Raymond was a major influence on modern Japanese architecture. He had, amongst a huge variety of work, designed supposedly earthquake and fire-proof homes for the Rising Sun Petroleum Company. At Dugway he faithfully reproduced construction methods and materials. Typical internal shoji paper doors, tatami mats and even sets of wooden chopsticks were part of the interiors. He was not, he wrote after the war, proud of his work at Dugway.

To build the German homes, the military brought in the Jewish émigré architect Erich Mendelsohn, best known for his expressionist Einstein Tower, a solar observatory in Potsdam which was used to prove Einstein's theory of relativity by measuring the sun's spectral lines. Other works had included a hat factory in Luckenwalde, numerous synagogues and grand department stores.

'The primary element is function. But function without a sensual component remains construction' was his guiding principle. Mendelsohn had left Germany in 1933 when Hitler came to power and settled first in England, where he designed the De La Warr Pavilion in Bexhill, before moving to the United States. Now charged with building replicas of the very homes he had known in Berlin so that the Allies could destroy them, he enlisted the help of German émigré set designers from the RKO studios in Hollywood. Once again, detail was of vital importance so the interiors included heavy German furniture, typical German clothing of the time in the cupboards, and children's toys on the floor.

Napalm trials at the Dugway Proving Ground in the Utah desert.

Prisoners at the nearby Utah State Prison were used as construction workers and both the German and Japanese replica homes were completed within six weeks. B-17 and B-24 bombers were primed and the experiments to identify the most effective incendiary devices set in motion. After each 'attack' the firebombed homes were attended by professional firefighters and the time it took to extinguish the fires carefully noted by scientists.

The longer it took the firefighters to bring the blaze under control, the more effective the incendiary devices were judged to be. The homes were then rebuilt with the same attention to detail as before. And the bombers came again with different payloads.

The most successful bomb to emerge from the experiments was the M-69 cluster bomb containing the napalm Fieser had produced with gasoline, naphthalene and the palmitic acid from coconuts. The M-74 bombs which contained coconut oil, rubber and gasoline were contenders but found to be less effective. With the tests completed the bomb-making got underway. In the first week of March 1945 more than 300 B-29 bombers were assembled on the American Mariana islands in the Western Pacific and loaded with the napalm cluster bombs. (A plan to attach mini incendiary devices with time fuses to the stomachs of thousands of bats which would nest in the rafters of enemy factories and warehouses was not followed through.) The B-29s were under the command of Air Force General Curtis LeMay. Tokyo could not possibly have contemplated what LeMay was about to unleash. He wanted a clear night with a decent wind to fan the inferno he was going to create. And towards the end of that first week in March he was handed the forecast he was waiting for. LeMay ordered the strike on Tokyo for the night of 9–10 March when strong winds were promised. Codenamed 'Operation Meetinghouse', the raid began in the early evening of 9 March when the first of the B-29 Superfortress long-range bombers climbed into the skies of the Western Pacific for the 1500-mile journey to the Japanese capital. The first wave of bombers arrived over the city under the cover of darkness, flying low to avoid the enemy's radar. The men, women and children of the Shitamachi district of Tokyo were woken by the drone of the bombers overhead and before they had time to dress, were engulfed in a deadly nightmare of raging fires and colossal heat. Homes, offices and factories had become an inferno in minutes. As the flames devoured oxygen thousands were asphyxiated before they were incinerated. Others were burned to death. Still more suffered burns that ate through huge areas of flesh. By the time the all-clear was sounded at around 5.00 a.m., the incendiary bombs had reduced a large part of Tokyo to piles of ash and smouldering flesh. Robert Guillan, a French reporter living in Tokyo at the time, described the prime target of factories, warehouses and workers' homes as having 'all the ingredients for creating a perfect fire storm'. More than 100,000 people died and a million were left homeless. It was not the coconut's finest hour. The US Air Force lost fourteen of their aircraft and crew. Sixteen square miles of Tokyo had been flattened. Katsumoto Saotome who survived the attack recalled how the napalm stuck to skin and burned the flesh right down to the bone. 'We scorched and boiled and baked to death more people in Tokyo on that night of March 9–10 than went up in vapor [*sic*] at Hiroshima and Nagasaki combined,' wrote General Curtis LeMay, who directed the Tokyo attack.

Louis Fieser's mixture of gasoline, naphthalene and acid from coconuts had done its job. But thirty years later Fieser wrote to President Nixon about the way the United States was using his invention in Indochina: 'It seems to me desirable,' he wrote, 'to try to promote an international agreement to outlaw further use of napalm or napalm-type munitions.' Fieser was concerned that napalm was being used to burn people as well as buildings. He claimed that when he was developing it he never thought of it as an anti-personnel weapon. But he got the brush-off from Nixon. However, Fieser never hid from his discovery of napalm. In 1972 he told Harvard's daily journal, *The Crimson*, that he had no reason to be ashamed of his work. But he remained adamantly against its use as an anti-personnel weapon. Nonetheless his image was sorely damaged as public opinion turned against his invention and lost sight of his pioneering work into cancer-producing cells and vitamin synthesis. He told the *New York Times* in 1967 that the contents of his mailbox could be summed up as, 'We thought you were a good guy, and now you're a bum.' Fieser responded by saying he could not have foreseen his napalm being used on 'babies and Buddhists'. He died in the summer of 1977 aged 78. The US Navy began the disposal of America's stockpile of incendiary bombs in 1994, and in 2009, on his first day in office, President Barack Obama signed a United Nations protocol banning the use of incendiary weapons.

While Fieser was at work in the chemistry labs at Harvard, a young John F. Kennedy was studying government and international relations on the other side of the university campus. Kennedy went on to Princeton to do postgraduate work while doing all he could to get into his country's naval reserve.

He succeeded in the end but, had it not been for coconuts, Kennedy's naval exploits might have put paid to his chances of becoming president of the United States or even living beyond his 20s. Kennedy loved the sea but, with his back problems and general poor health, stood little chance of passing any military fitness exam. But his father Joseph had been ambassador in London when Alan Clark was the naval attaché. By 1941 Clark had become Director of US Naval Intelligence, and a word from Kennedy senior in Clark's ear saw to it that Kennedy junior was accepted by the Naval Reserve in October of that same year – just two months before the Japanese bombed the US fleet in Hawaii's Pearl Harbor.

Kennedy proved himself an able recruit and progressed through naval intelligence to the motor torpedo boat squadron and its operations in the South Pacific. It was the spring of 1943. The Japanese had occupied islands in the Solomons during the first half of 1942 with a view to interrupting the allied supply lines between Australia, New Zealand and the United States. By 1943 the Japanese had captured the strategically important island of

Lieutenant John Kennedy in his motor torpedo boat in 1943. (US Navy)

Tulagi in the southern Solomons. From there they established garrisons throughout the central and northern islands, seriously interfering with the allied supply routes. The allies launched a two-part counter-offensive. A combined air group – the Cactus Air Force – was established and based at Henderson Field on the island of Guadalcanal. At the same time squadrons of motor torpedo boats were based at islands held by the allies from where they launched raids on the Japanese supply ships and their escorts.

Kennedy was by then 26, a lieutenant and in charge of patrol torpedo (PT) boat 109 operating from its base on the island of Lumbari. His boat was one of fifteen patrolling the Blackett Strait, south of Kolombangara on the night of 1 August when a convoy of Japanese supply ships, with destroyers as escorts, approached the strait under full steam. The PT boats fired thirty torpedoes without making a significant impact on the enemy ships. Twelve of the torpedo boats had spent their ammunition and were ordered to return to base to reload. PT109 and two others remained on station. It was a moonless, starless night, still and pitch black. By early morning on 2 August, PT109 and her crew had still failed to find any of the Japanese ships. Kennedy was at the helm. Dawn was still three hours away.

Nobody heard it coming. Out of the blackness and cruising at more than 30 knots, a Japanese destroyer was suddenly on 109's starboard bow. Kennedy yelled instructions to his crew as he attempted to turn his boat so that the torpedoes were lined up ready to be fired at the enemy ship. But the destroyer, the *Amagiri*, was moving too fast, towering over them and closing at terrifying speed. It was too late. The *Amagiri* smashed into the American boat, splitting it in two. Kennedy was thrown across the cockpit. Two of his crew, Harold Marney and Andrew Kirksey, died instantly. Fire broke out and there was imminent danger of an explosion as leaking oil spilled from the boat's fuel tanks. Kennedy ordered his crew to abandon ship. One man, Patrick McMahon his engineer, was already severely burned, and gunner's mate Charles Harris sustained serious injuries to his leg.

In the water, they waited for the inevitable. But the destroyer was seemingly oblivious of the collision. What's more, its wash dispersed the burning oil and the danger of an explosion passed. So, making sure all the living members of his crew were accounted for, Kennedy ordered everyone back to what was left of their wrecked craft. From there he took stock. But as they clung to the remains of their boat it began to sink. There was a small island barely visible (3 miles away, as it turned out) which Kennedy judged to be their best bet. The water was flat again which made swimming easier. Kennedy towed the injured McMahon with the strap of the man's life jacket in his teeth. The others looked after themselves keeping an eye on Harris who was struggling with his injured leg. Their life jackets gave them buoyancy and from time to time they would tread water to regain some energy. But the fear of more Japanese ships kept them going, and after five hours the eleven exhausted survivors crawled up the beach.

Their island refuge proved a disappointment. It was at least free of Japanese which had not been taken for granted. But it was a barren island with nothing to eat or drink. The men's spirits began to flag. McMahon and Harris were in considerable pain and needed medical attention. Overhead, Japanese 'Betty' bombers were streaming towards the allied air base at Henderson field. Kennedy and his friend George Ross, who had joined 109's crew on the fateful night, took to the water again (at Harvard, Kennedy had been in the swimming team) in the hope of spotting friendly ships. But there were none to be seen.

From the water, Kennedy and Ross had spotted a second, larger island on which there seemed to be coconut palms, which promised both food and drink. If they stayed where they were they would all starve to death. But fatigue made more hours in the water a desperate alternative. They sat in silence. Despair began to cloud the men's eyes. Kennedy himself was exhausted but in time managed to struggle to his feet. They all knew what had to be done and took Kennedy's move as their signal. With a few words of encouragement, he led his men back into the water. Once again, he towed McMahon while Ross kept an eye on the others. The coconut palms were soon clearly visible, turning despair into hope, and with hope came a final burst of energy. Incredibly, everyone survived the journey. The coconuts were plentiful, providing both food and drink, while the palms provided shade. But the ordeal for Kennedy and his men was far from over. They were stranded on a Pacific island with no means of communication and with the risk of being discovered by a Japanese patrol. Once again it fell to Kennedy and his friend George Ross to find the answers. A third island had been identified and several of the men claimed to see signs of life. That was good news if they turned out to be indigenous islanders – the islanders were already on the side of the allies, having suffered at the hands of the Japanese – but it would be very bad news if those distant figures turned out to be enemy troops.

Rested and nourished, Kennedy and Ross went back into the water. With new-found energy they were soon within striking distance of the third island's beach. And they had struck lucky: the islanders who came to greet them were indeed friendly and anxious to help. After polite introductions, Kennedy tried valiantly to explain their predicament. He and Ross and their nine crew members still on the island across the water needed to get back to their base at Rendova. Two of their number needed urgent medical treatment. But the two islanders, Eroni Kumana and Biuku Gasa, had no English, and little of what Kennedy was saying made any sense to them. They did, however, know about the allied base at Rendova. It would be a hazardous trip by canoe across waters patrolled by the Japanese but Kumana and Gasa indicated they were willing to take the risk. That was a start. But with no English, their chances of convincing the base commanders they were genuine and then being able to explain where to find the American crew were slim. Kennedy could write a note indicating their position, but if their new-found friends were intercepted by a Japanese patrol, they would be charged as collaborators and the crew of PT109 would be picked up and taken prisoner.

But a canoe with two native islanders and some coconuts would hardly raise any suspicions. Kennedy grabbed a coconut and scrubbed the shell clean. With a knife he then began to carve a message into the shell, taking care that Kumana and Gasa could see clearly what he was doing. The result looked as though some child had been writing a 'been here' missive for future beachcombers. The real message, however, was very clear:

'NAURO ISL COMMANDER NATIVE KNOWS POS'IT HE CAN PILOT 11 ALIVE NEED SMALL BOAT KENNEDY'

Kennedy handed the inscribed coconut to Kumana. 'Rendova,' said Kennedy. Nothing more needed saying. The two natives collected food and water, carried their dugout canoe down to the water's edge and with brief handshakes and encouraging smiles from the weary sailors, set out on their mission.

Under the coconut palms and out of sight of enemy patrols on the water and in the air, the Americans waited and waited, fearing for the two islanders and fearing for themselves. The grey/pink of dusk joined the sea to the sky on the horizon. Then total darkness. At dawn there was still no sign of the canoe and hopes began to fade. Until, and at first they were unsure, there was something in the distance, low on the water. Gradually the outline of two human forms became clear, then the shape of the canoe and at last the paddles plunging into the water. The welcoming party at the water's edge found the canoe full of provisions and hidden amongst the provisions a note from the base commander. A rescue plan was taking shape. For Kumana and Gasa there was a hero's welcome (Kennedy subsequently invited them to Washington) and there was much celebrating amongst the crew. Their ordeal had run into its sixth day. But Kennedy was impatient and persuaded Ross to join him in the islanders' canoe to look for friendly ships. An account of what happened next is lodged in the Kennedy library:

> Heavy seas swamped the canoe and so battered the men that they barely made it back to Naru. But the next morning, August 7, eight islanders appeared at Naru shortly after Kennedy and Ross awoke. They brought food and instructions from the local Allied coastwatcher, Lt. A. Reginald Evans, who instructed Kennedy to come to Evans's post.
>
> Stopping long enough at Olasana to feed the crew, the islanders hid Kennedy under a pile of palm fronds and paddled him to Gomu Island in Blackett Strait. Early in the evening of August 7, a little more than six days after PT-109's sinking, Kennedy

stepped on to Gomu. There was still a rescue to be planned with Evans, no small thing in enemy-held waters, but the worst of the ordeal of PT 109 was over.

Evans already notified his commander of the discovery of PT-109's survivors, and the base commander proposed sending a rescue mission directly to Olasana. Kennedy insisted on being picked up first so that he could guide the rescue boats, PT 157 and PT 171, among the reefs and shallows of the island chain. Late on the night of August 7, the boats met Kennedy at the rendezvous point, exchanging a prearranged signal of four shots. Kennedy's revolver was down to only three rounds, so he borrowed a rifle from Evans for the fourth. Standing up in the canoe to give the signal, Kennedy did not anticipate the rifle's recoil, which threw him off balance and dumped him in the water. A soaking wet and thoroughly exasperated Navy lieutenant climbed aboard PT 157.

The PT boats crossed Blackett Strait under Kennedy's direction and eased up to Olasana Island early in the morning of August 8. The exhausted men of PT 109 were all asleep. Kennedy began yelling for them, much to the chagrin of his rescuers, who were nervous about the proximity of the Japanese. But the rescue went forward without incident, and the men of PT 109 reached the US base at Rendova at 5:30 a.m. on August 8.

Kennedy moved in to the White House in 1961. Nine months later ships carrying Soviet missiles were detected en route for Cuba, plunging the world into the seminal crisis of the Cold War. Anyone doubting the young president's resolve in facing down the Soviets would have been reassured by glancing across the Oval Office desk. On it, mounted on a wood and plastic base, stood the coconut shell with its wartime message. It remained there throughout Kennedy's presidency.

Queen Victoria's subjects in the South Pacific should have been enjoying a sun-blessed and peaceful existence. But the Gilbert Islanders were the most warlike of the Micronesians whose bitter and violent disputes were usually the result of political rivalry, revenge for murder, and arguments over land and women. The most fearsome warriors, from Kiribati and Nauru, wielded shark-tooth spears and vicious hand weapons of various styles and lengths made from mature coconut timber. As defence against these weapons the warriors had developed complete body armour consisting of a suit woven from heavy strands of coconut fibre. Lengths of this coir were placed on top of one another, each one was covered with two-ply twisted, coir cords.

The individual ribs were covered and secured in place by interlinking coir cords. The sides of the cuirass culminated in a waistband which was tightened and secured by plaited coir ties. A panel of similar construction was attached to the back using an internal wooden support as a neck and head guard. It had a wide flap at the back that curved up and forward, protecting the back of the head. This guard was intended to protect the back of the head from any misdirected efforts of the women of the party who followed the men into the fight, throwing stones at the enemy. This armour not only protected the wearer but also served to catch and break the teeth of his antagonists' weapon. In battle each armoured man was accompanied by one or more unarmoured 'squires' who acted as skirmishers until the battle proper was joined, then stood behind their armoured masters passing them new weapons as needed. To give themselves added protection, the warriors wore knotted coconut-fibre leggings, and helmets made of the skin of a porcupine fish with its quill-like spines intact.

Former warriors from the Kiribati islands that straddle the equator in the South Pacific, armed with shark teeth swords, wear coir armour and fish skin helmets.

Some 1,300 miles south west across the South Pacific, coir armour would have come in handy during the Coconut War of 1980 which brought British and French colonialists head to head in the New Hebrides. This colonial outpost, a group of some eighty coconut-exporting islands 1,500 miles east of Queensland, had been run jointly by Britain and France since 1906. Britain held the islands on the strength of a 1774 claim by Captain Cook. The French ignored this fact, opened a trading company and shipped out settlers. By 1900 the islands were heavily stacked with French settlers, and to avoid trouble the British agreed to joint management six years later. It might have been thought that there were enough islands in the South Pacific for the two European powers to take their pick without treading on each other's toes. Coconut copra was and still is the main cash crop, and both the British and the French fancied the New Hebrides and refused to budge as independence approached. The two European administrations ran separate legal, educational and security systems in an atmosphere of mutual dislike.

Five years after claiming the New Hebrides for Britain, James Cook was on his third and last voyage of discovery when he entered Kealakekua Bay on the west coast of Hawaii with his ships the *Resolution* and *Discovery*. His welcome from the islanders was tumultuous and Cook himself was afforded all manner of honours. According to journals kept by members of his crew, a young, bearded island priest called Kaireekea chewed some coconut and having made it into a paste with his saliva proceeded to smear it over Cook's head, face and arms. This was followed by a lavish feast which included a coconut pudding. Cook had made a point of eating anything islanders offered him but mindful of the sight and smell of a decaying pig which had accompanied earlier prayers found he had lost his appetite. The sight of pork was just too much. 'He (Cook) could not get a morsel down,' observed James King in his journal, 'not even when the old fellow (his host) very politely chewed it for him.'

Andrew Stuart, the son of a clergyman who became Bishop of Uganda, was a foreign office stalwart with years of colonial administration under his belt. He was Britain's commissioner, based on Santo Espiritu, the largest of the eighty islands of the New Hebrides. He arrived there in 1978, with the brief of bringing independence to the island colony. Each district in the volcanic outcrops scattered over 500 miles of sea had two government agents, one British, one French. Disputes were many but largely petty.

At 6ft 7in Stuart towered over his French opposite number, Inspecteur-General Jean-Jacques Robert, a veteran of the Free French Forces and himself an experienced colonial administrator. The two occupied separate residencies – the French used a two-storey, white-painted building in the capital, Port Vila, while Stuart and his team occupied a bungalow perched above the harbour on Iririki Island. Relations between the two European powers in the islands were cool, to say the least. Elections held in 1979 during the run-up to independence returned English speakers to the ruling assembly with a two-thirds majority on all the islands including Santo Espiritu. The winning party was Vanuaaku Pati, led by an Anglican priest, Father Walter Lini. But Jimmy Stevens, the leader of a group of French-speaking rebels encouraged by the Frenchman Robert, who had liaised with Stevens behind Stuart's back, refused to accept this outcome. Tempting his bow-and-arrow-wielding followers with the promise of women, modern gadgets and vehicles but not necessarily in that order, Stevens, a truck driver who had reportedly fathered forty-two children, established the rebel republic of Vemarana.

Stuart and Monsieur Robert were supposedly jointly steering the islands (current population 250,000) towards independence scheduled for the end of July in 1980. But France was loath to leave and, when Britain insisted, gave covert support to a rebellion of French settlers led by Stevens who was persuaded to block the airport, blow up a few bridges and overthrow the local colonial-led police. Law enforcement agencies loyal to the islands' new Prime Minister Lini put down the rebellion in a skirmish that lasted a few hours, but not before Jimmy Stevens had been arrested and his son killed. At Stuart's request, British Prime Minister Margaret Thatcher sent 200 marines who were met on the beach by near-naked rebels (gourds covered their penises) carrying spears and bows and arrows.

Faced with the firepower of the British commandos, the rebels, finding their courage had deserted them, threw down their weapons, clutched their gourds and retreated into the safety of the jungle. Foreign newspapers could not resist calling the rebellion the Coconut War. The New Hebrides gained their independence and adopted the name Vanuatu.

Of the two men who had steered the New Hebrides to independence, Mr Lini died in 1999 but not before he had played a significant role in putting an end to French nuclear tests in the region. Andrew Stuart, who had outflanked his French opposite number, went on to be Britain's ambassador in Finland. He died in 2014 at the age of 86. Two companies, Coconut Oil Production Santo Ltd and Vanuatu Virgin Coconut Oil, both based in Luganville, the capital of Santu Espiritu, dominate Vanuatu's coconut business, producing both oil and animal feed. And research is ongoing into using the oil as an alternative to diesel and petrol.

5

IN SICKNESS AND IN HEALTH

Four popes have died of malaria. Giambattista Castana, who was elected Pope Urban VII in 1590, would have been the fifth had he not died of the disease before his coronation. Killer mosquitoes had thrived in the Pontine marshes south of Rome for centuries until Mussolini ordered the marshes to be drained when he became Italy's prime minister in 1922. (The word malaria comes from the Italian *mal aria* bad air.) The Germans flooded the marshes during their occupation in the Second World War triggering a new outbreak of malaria which killed hundreds of Italian civilians. George Washington and George Clooney succumbed, and Michael Caine was infected with cerebral malaria in Korea. August Engelhardt, the German nudist and cocovore (one who eats nothing but coconuts) contracted the disease on his unspoiled Eden in the South Seas. Bats, snakes and apes contract malaria, and biologists are speculating that dinosaurs might have suffered too.

According to the World Health Organisation, malaria infects more than 200 million people every year: in 2016 an estimated 445,000 sufferers died of the disease. Sub-Saharan Africa accounts for 90 per cent of cases, with children under 5 and pregnant women being most at risk. Discarded coconut halves that collect water have proved to be an ideal breeding ground for the mosquito responsible for transmitting malaria. Various methods preventing the mosquito from attacking its victims are used to varying degrees of success. But a vaccine for malaria has so far proved hard to find, not least because the malaria parasite *plasmodium falciparum* consists of more than 5,000 genes. (In comparison, the polio virus, for example, is comprised of just eleven genes.) This makes a vaccine hard to design, although a research company in Maryland now claims that clinical trials in Equatorial Guinea of its new drug could lead to the commercial production of a vaccine by 2020.

For centuries, and up until the 1940s, it was quinine that provided treatment for malaria sufferers. Seventeenth-century Jesuit priests in Peru – Jesuits were prevented from studying medicine lest it divert their attention from matters spiritual, but were nonetheless accomplished apothecaries – were the first to isolate quinine from the bark of the cinchona tree. They called their new find *quina quina* (bark of barks). Samples were sent to Rome, a city of swamps and marshes in the 1700s where malaria was endemic. It was so effective that the people of Rome could not help but describe it as the miracle drug, a sentiment with which seventeenth-century popes happily concurred, creating a huge and spiralling demand for the bark.

Three centuries later in the 1930s Paul Muller, a Swiss chemist, produced *dichloro-diphenyl-trichloroethane* or DDT which proved highly effective against all kinds of insects including mosquitoes. It won Herr Muller a Nobel prize for medicine. But his DDT was snapped up by farmers the world over. It was cheap and the farmers used too much of it, turning what had been a life saver into a pollutant. The malaria eradication programme was halted and DDT eventually withdrawn from the market. To make matters worse for parts of the world where malaria is endemic, the malarial parasite was outsmarting every other insecticide put in its way.

But Palmira Ventosilla would outsmart the mosquitoes – with coconuts. Professor Ventosilla is a microbiologist at the Alexander von Humboldt Tropical Medicine Institute in Lima, Peru. Peru had given the world quinine; it was about to provide the world with an ingenious follow-up. Professor Ventosilla had followed the work of a group of researchers who had surveyed mosquito-breeding sites in Israel. They were looking for natural pathogens and parasites that attacked the mosquito larvae and found a new strain of the *Bacillus thuringiensis* bacterium which they isolated from a stagnant pond near the Zeelim Kibbutz in the Negev Desert. They named it *Bacillus thuringiensis israelensis* or Bti.

What Professor Ventosilla did was to put Bti together with coconuts. There were areas in the north of Peru where malaria was a serious problem. These areas were characterised by numerous fish ponds and narrow irrigation canals. The problem was finding a way for local people to apply the Bti. There were plenty of coconuts and Ventosilla knew that coconuts contained the amino acids and carbohydrates that support Bti. And while Bti was toxic for seventy-two species of mosquito by killing the larvae, it was harmless to fish, birds, mammals and humans.

In her lab, Ventosilla introduced a small quantity of Bti into a mature coconut through a small hole that she then plugged with cotton and sealed with candle wax. The hard shell of the coconut protects the incubating *bacillus*, and the water inside contains the amino acids and carbohydrates necessary for its reproduction. After two or three days of fermentation, the coconuts were taken to ponds where the mosquitoes were known to live, the plugs removed and the coconuts thrown into the stagnant pools of water. Two or three coconuts were used to cover a typical pond.

For twelve days, eight ponds in Salitral, a small town in the north of Peru with a population of around 6,000, were almost entirely free of mosquito larva, their numbers decimated by the *Bacillus thuringiensis israelensis* that had escaped from the coconuts. So far so good. But Ventosilla and her small team were not about to travel the world with a bunch of coconuts in their luggage. Local communities in malaria-infected regions would have to do the work themselves. So she put together a Bti do-it-yourself kit, and designed an education programme for schools and local communities. The kits contain a cotton swab seeded with 1,000–10,000 Bti spores, another swab with 40mg of sodium glutamate, a small piece of cotton and instructions on how to inoculate the coconut. With it, anyone, even those with a basic education, could inoculate a coconut, wait for the Bti population to grow suitably potent, and then open the coconut and toss it into a pond.

These biological coconut bombs are harmless to humans and to most other organisms. The World Health Organisation (WHO) issued a guideline saying that even in drinking water, Bti is not known to be harmful to people. But it is lethal to the mosquito including the *Aedes aegypti* variety that carries the zika virus. Word of the coconut bombs spread. Ventosilla took her simple science to Guyana, while scientists in Indonesia followed her example with their own teams and their home-grown nuts. Deaths from malaria have fallen 29 per cent since 2010 according to the WHO, although it has to be said that the coconut bombs cannot claim the credit for more than a percentage point or two of that decline.

The coconut's role in health care is nothing new. The rise of Islam in the second half of the first century brought a thirst for knowledge and an early systematic approach to drugs in Damascus at the court of the ruling Umayyads. Coconut camphor, senna, aloes and aconite were all believed to possess medicinal qualities. One alchemist reported that the coconut meat was 'astringent and it increases the semen'. Sudden and unexplained deaths were not uncommon at court and were regularly attributed to poison, persuading the Umayyad leaders of the need to identify the poisons and find cures for them. The alchemists of the period were obliged to concentrate their researches in toxicology, an area in which a Christian pharmacist Ibn Uthal was regarded highly. But neither Uthal nor the alchemists in Damascus thought to produce any coconut charcoal. Had they done so, the death rate as a result of ingested poisons could have been radically reduced. As it happened, several centuries were to pass before doctors discovered how effective coconut could be as an antidote to poisons.

When coconuts first arrived in Europe in the fifteenth century, they came packed on Venetian galleys, along with luxuries such as silks and sugar and stacked next to exotic pets such as monkeys and parrots. And they came with the promise of healing all manner of bodily malfunctions, from digestive disorders to haemorrhoids. The Venetians had brought them from Alexandria, and the nut's distant and exotic home together with its size – it was many times bigger than any other nut – suggested supernatural powers at a time when science had yet to inform the management of medical problems.

It was the age when the lack of medical science necessitated using homespun remedies – often including an array of herbs – to treat everything from toothache to tonsillitis. These remedies were nothing if not exotic. Sciatica, or back pain, might be treated by taking:

> a spoonful of the gall of a red ox and two spoonfuls of water-pepper and four of the patient's urine, and as much cumin as half a French nut and as much suet as a small nut and break and bruise your cumin. Boil these together till they be like gruel

> then let him lay his haunch bone [hip] against the fire as hot as he may bear it and anoint [sic] him with the same ointment for a quarter of an hour or half a quarter, and then clap on a hot cloth folded five or six times and at night lay a hot sheet folded many times to the spot and let him lie still two or three days and he shall not feel pain but be well.

For burns the advice was down to earth: 'Take a live snail and rub its slime against the burn and it will heal.' (Recent research has in fact shown that snail slime contains antioxidants, antiseptic, anaesthetic, anti-irritant, anti-inflammatory, antibiotic and anti-viral properties, as well as collagen and elastin, vital for skin repair.)

For haemorrhoids the suggestion was to use coconut oil, and for digestive problems the pure water of the young green coconut was the answer. Both were very probably effective. Coconut oil is recommended today by alternative medicine practitioners for haemorrhoids (and for various skin complaints), and the coconut's water was pure and clean which was more than could be said of the water most people were drinking. On top of which the white flesh of the coconut helped to put on weight for those who were seriously under-nourished. It also helped, as the alchemists in Damascus had suggested, to increase the volume of semen.

A fifteenth-century painting of an apothecary in Modena, Italy shows a coconut on the table. By the sixteenth century, coconuts were available at apothecaries throughout Italy according to the physician and botanist Pietro Andrea Mattioli who produced the encyclopaedia of Renaissance pharmacology. (He also happened to be the first scientist to recognise people could be allergic to cats.) The coconut had found its place in the medicine cupboard – or at least on top of it.

The few doctors there were at the time treated only the rich. Some of these doctors had received medical qualifications from the first European medical school established in the eleventh century at Salerno in Italy, or from those set up later at Bologna and Montpellier in France. Through these medical schools, the doctors of Europe began to learn about the ideas of Arabic and ancient Greek medicine. Pharmacies in Baghdad had been doing business since the ninth century, prescribing coconut, rhubarb, musk, nutmeg, cloves and tamarind. Compared to the knowledge of the Arabs, European medicine was not very advanced. A Syrian writer describes how two doctors – one Arab the other European – argued about how to treat an abscess, an infected lump on a knight's leg. The Arab prepared a dressing with ointment to open the lump and draw out the infection. The European insisted the only thing to do was to cut the leg off.

Most people in medieval Europe never saw a doctor – a fact that some might say was in their favour. They were treated by the local wise-woman who was skilled in the use of herbs, or by the priest, or the barber who pulled out teeth, set broken bones and performed other operations. Their cures were a mixture of superstition and herbal remedies including coconuts. Monks and nuns ran hospitals in their monasteries and convents which took in the sick and dying.

As the treatment of infections and other medical disorders became science based, the coconut's usefulness as a medicine waned. But as medical science developed, researchers began to look again at the venerable nut, and discovered that some of those early treatments were supported by what science was suggesting, not least of all the use of coconut charcoal – the charcoal produced by burning nut shells. The first recorded use of charcoal for medicinal purposes comes from Egyptian papyri around 1500 BC. The principal use appears to have been to adsorb the unpleasant odours from putrefying wounds and from within the intestinal tract. Hippocrates (*c.* 400 BC), and then Pliny (AD 50), recorded the use of charcoal for treating a wide range of complaints including epilepsy, chlorosis (a severe form of iron-deficiency anaemia), vertigo, and anthrax. Pliny writes in his epoch-defining, thirty-seven-volume work *Natural History*:

> It is only when ignited and quenched that charcoal itself acquires its characteristic powers, and only when it seems to have perished that it becomes endowed with greater virtue.

What Pliny observed and noted so long ago is at the heart of what science continues to exploit today.

There was however a long gap before coconut charcoal gained a firm place in the minds of doctors and surgeons. But when it did, its uses became widespread. By the mid-1800s charcoal had become a well-known treatment for a number of health conditions. James Bird, an army surgeon, recorded his observations in 1857:

> … Charcoal mixed with bread crumbs or yeast, has long been a favourite material for forming poultices, among army and navy surgeons. The charcoal poultice has also obtained a high character in hospital practice as an application to sloughing ulcers and gangrenous sores, and recently, this substance has afforded immense relief in numerous cases of open cancer, by soothing pain, correcting foetor, and facilitating the separation of the morbid structure from the surrounding parts. It is unnecessary to mention other instances of its utility; for in this form Charcoal is now admitted into the London Pharmacopoeia, and it is in general use in all naval, military, and civil hospitals …

The development of the charcoal activation process by which the adsorbent powers of the charcoal are greatly enhanced, saw doctors using the activated charcoal orally as an antidote for poisons and as a cure for intestinal disorders. Modern medicine continues to use activated charcoal to treat ingested poisons. It performs in exactly the same way as it does in gas masks, and in the nuclear fusion reactor, adsorbing the poisons onto its surface. In the 1980s, researchers in the Department of Clinical Pharmacology at the University of Helsinki noted that:

> Activated charcoal has an ability to adsorb a wide variety of substances. Single doses of oral activated charcoal effectively prevent the gastrointestinal absorption of most drugs and toxins present in the stomach at the time of charcoal administration. Known exceptions are alcohols, cyanide, and metals such as iron and lithium. In general, activated charcoal is more effective than gastric emptying … Repeated dosing with oral activated charcoal enhances the elimination of many toxicologically significant agents. It also accelerates the elimination of many industrial and environmental intoxicants. To avoid delays in charcoal administration, activated charcoal should be a part of first-aid kits both at home and at work. The 'blind' administration of charcoal neither prevents later gastric emptying nor does it cause serious adverse effects provided that pulmonary aspiration in obtunded patients [patients having diminished mental awareness] is prevented. In severe acute poisonings oral activated charcoal should be administered repeatedly.

Self-harming patients will have discovered that activated coconut charcoal can be a very effective treatment for drug overdoses if administered within the hour of the drug being taken. The drug, with much else in the digestive tract, sticks to the porous surface of the charcoal and is excreted in what become very black stools. (Doctors warn that patients taking prescribed medications and offered charcoal should bear in mind that the charcoal will adsorb those prescribed drugs as well as the poison.) In emergency rooms throughout the United States activated coconut charcoal is commonly used as a first step in the treatment of ingested poisons and overdoses, and health professionals advise families with young children to keep a supply of charcoal in the cupboard at home.

The charcoal's ability to adsorb odours found a use in controlling the smell of rotting flesh in nineteenth-century hospitals, and today it is used in dressings when wound odours are distressing to the patient and/or relatives. It has wider uses too: dealing with farting is one of them. The NHS in England and Wales approves the use of activated charcoal 'to relieve the symptoms of indigestion, flatulence and hyperacidity. Clothing containing activated charcoal or charcoal pads placed inside clothing can help adsorb foul-smelling gas released during flatulence.'

Coconut charcoal is also gaining ground with face mask manufacturers. Masks, already a popular accessory for commuters in Japan, are fast becoming an essential part of every city cyclist's protective wear. (The Japanese wear masks to keep their own germs from spreading; to prevent inhaling the germs of others; to filter the pollutants of urban life; to cover perceived facial imperfections; to hide emotion; as a fashion item; and just to be in step with what everyone else is doing.) One mask manufacturer in the United States has updated its sales pitch by announcing that 'Instead of bituminous coal, the new carbon layer is a cellulose base containing military grade steam activated carbon from coconut shells with no additional substances.'

While the benefits of coconut charcoal are well established, the health benefits of coconut oil are far from proven although claims to the contrary abound. If wellness websites are to be believed, coconut oil could halve the NHS drugs bill and ensure everyone's maiden aunt would live arthritis-free to 100 without the slightest fear of contracting Alzheimer's. The claims made for the oil are astonishing. One American nutritionist lists the following benefits on his website:

Prevents heart disease and high blood pressure
Cures kidney infection and UTI (Urinary tract infection)
Reduces inflammation and arthritis
Prevents and treats cancer
Boosts the immune system
Improves memory and brain function
Improves energy and endurance

Improves digestion, reduces ulcers and colitis
Helps gall bladder disease and pancreatitis
Improves skin issues
Prevents gum disease and tooth decay
Proven Alzheimer's disease natural treatment
Prevents osteoporosis
Improves type 2 diabetes
Helps weight loss
Builds muscles and decreases body fat
Benefits hair health
Fights candida and yeast infections
Balances hormones
Anti-aging [*sic*]

But science does not underwrite these astonishing and brazen claims for the oil's powers to prevent medical conditions. And there is scant information to suggest the oil even alleviates any of the cited ailments. And rather than exercising caution, competitive websites add a few more claims for good measure:

Acts as a sunscreen
Relieves stress
Soothes irritation on nursing nipples
Treats lice when mixed with apple cider vinegar

In cash-strapped Venezuela where medicines of all types from painkillers to cancer drugs are in short supply, these wild promises have found favour in a desperate population. A sharp increase in demand for coconut water, more usually mixed locally with whisky, reflects the belief that it has both antiviral and antibacterial properties. But the suggestion that the oil will 'prevent heart disease and high blood pressure' and at the same time can 'prevent and treat cancer' will stretch the imagination even of the most desperate Venezuelans.

To be fair, coconut oil is included in some NHS-approved skin creams where it typically forms the emollient base: the use of the oil in various forms is recognised for the treatment of psoriasis. Irish scientists have shown that the oil will attack the bacteria that cause caries (tooth decay). They found that enzyme-modified coconut oil effectively inhibited the growth of the bacteria *Streptococcus mutans*, a major cause of tooth decay. The lead researcher of the Irish team, Dr Damien Brady, told the *British Dental Journal* that 'incorporating enzyme modified coconut oil into dental hygiene products would be an attractive alternative to chemical additives.'

Tooth decay is one thing: keeping the teeth pearly white by 'pulling' is something else. Pulling is the process of swilling coconut oil around the mouth. Why 'pulling'? Because it is supposed that the oil 'pulls' plaque from the teeth. Dentists say there is no proof that it does. But purveyors of the oil and countless so-called celebrities insist it works:

> Oil pulling has been proven to be an effective method in reducing plaque formation and plaque induced gingivitis. This preliminary study shows that coconut oil is an easily usable, safe and cost-effective agent with minimal side effects which can be used as an adjuvant in oral hygiene maintenance,' says one group of researchers.

Hollywood actress Gwyneth Paltrow leads the oil-pulling celebrities. And in these early years of the twenty-first century, what so-called celebrities say matters – a state of affairs given succour by the growing lack of confidence in what 'experts' in general have to say. 'People in this country have had enough of experts,' Michael Gove, a Conservative politician, told the British people during the Brexit debate.

However, not everyone wants their teeth pearly white. Lieutenant Henry Townsend Somerville served on HMS *Penguin*, a naval survey ship carrying out duties in the South Pacific in the

1890s. Somerville became fascinated by the cultures of the South Seas islanders and began collecting artefacts that reflected the lives of those people he met ashore. One such item, now at Oxford University's Pitt Rivers Museum, is a coconut shell with primitive carvings painted red and white. According to Somerville, the coconut shell contained *noti*, a dark paste made of crushed stone and leaves. The paste was smeared on teeth to blacken them. Apparently shiny black teeth were considered attractive among the Solomon Islanders, and the nut container was probably carried around by the smart set who wanted their black-teeth smile to shine all day (see the bottom image on page 15 of the picture section). Teeth blackening was also used in make-up for women in Thailand, Laos and Japan to protect their teeth from decay and in part as a fashion statement. Perversely, women in Renaissance Europe painted healthy teeth black to make it look as though the teeth were rotten. Sugar tended to rot the teeth and it was only the rich who could afford sugar. So teeth that looked rotten served as a convincing status symbol.

Twenty-first-century celebrities continue to spread their influence, and it is not just what they say, it is what they do and how they invest their money. A lot of that money followed two friends into a bar on New York's Lower East Side back in 2003. Michael Kirban and Ira Liran had been friends since high school. Kirban had dropped out of college and was running a software company he had set up with his father. Liran, who had a degree from Columbia University in Italian cultural studies, was selling Italian jewellery. Both had an eye for a pretty woman. In that Lower East Side bar they struck up a conversation with two women visiting from Brazil, and Ira fell head-over-heels in love with one of them.

Business gurus would countenance against love being a safe or even sensible basis for a new enterprise. However, in the course of that romantic evening it transpired that what the two Brazilian women missed most about home was coconut water. As Ira's heartstrings hit the high notes, the popularity of coconut water in Brazil was ringing a few bells with Michael.

When Ira followed his heart and jumped on a plane to Brazil, Michael put his entrepreneurial brain into gear. The cogs flew and a few months later, with a plan in his back pocket, Michael paid Ira and his new girlfriend a visit. Kirban laid out his plans on the beach at Buzios, where a bronzed, pouting Brigitte Bardot sits ruefully gazing out to sea. (She had put the upscale resort east of Rio on the map in the 1960s.) Before the sun went down, the two men had come to an agreement on launching a coconut water business in the United States, and fifteen years later that business was the world's leading brand of coconut water in a market worth some US $3 billion.

The demand for this new 'health' drink has grown with astonishing speed, thanks in part to some savvy marketing. It does have a distinctive flavour unlike plain spring water. It contains plenty of electrolytes and lacks the calories of so-called sports drinks. So it is good for rehydration. (In remote tropical hospitals where doctors run short of saline drips, pure coconut water from young nuts, with its sodium and potassium and small quantities of other electrolytes, is used intravenously as a rehydrating agent. It was a common standby in field hospitals during the war in the Pacific.) But you need to have done some pretty tough exercising and for an hour or more to require the kind of rehydration coconut water offers. Tap water or plain bottled water will do for most people. And do it cheaper. This did not worry Kirban and Liran. They had a vision. They sourced a coconut water supplier right there in Brazil, bought enough to fill two ships' containers, did a hasty deal with Tetra Pak and booked their cartons of *Vita Coco* onto a freighter bound for the promised land they believed New York to be … But a vital part of US import regulations had slipped their minds, and three days before their ship was due to dock they had a call from the Food and Drug Administration (FDA) asking for their new product's registration number. They had not applied for one, and an application would take eighteen weeks to process.

Some would have panicked, others would have drowned their sorrows in something much stronger than coconut water. Michael and Ira did neither. Their ship's schedule offered an opportunity. They worked the phones frantically and in the nick of time managed to get their containers offloaded in the Bahamas. Kirban met the ship as it docked in Nassau.

He hired a roomy hatchback and set about hawking his wares round the bars, hotels and clubs. Short, with a shaven head, a silver tongue and plenty of entrepreneurial spirit, Kirban worked the city of offshore bankers with remarkable success, getting rid of half the consignment and breaking even. Three months later he had his certificate from the FDA and was overseeing his first consignment of *Vita Coco* to be unloaded at the docks in New York. No rental cars this time. Kirban put on his skates, strapped a huge bag of cartons to his back and as darkness fell, swooped around the bars and cafes of the Big Apple. He made his calls at night, he told *The New York Times*, because the owners were there counting their money and it was the owners he needed to target.

This one-man marketing initiative was having considerable success and *Vita Coco* was receiving an encouraging reception until the manager of a health products store dropped a bombshell. He told Kirban that his was not the only brand of coconut water to be doing the rounds. Mark Rampulla, a one-time Peace Corps worker who had developed a taste for coconut water in Costa Rica, had just begun selling his own brand calling it *Zico*. On the streets of Manhattan war broke out – a dirty war at that. According to *The New York Times*, it was Rampulla's *Zico* that took first blood when it gained entry to a small but upscale chain of yoga studios. *Vita Coco* secured the business at Whole Foods

Market in Union Square and when *Zico* arrived competition tactics got nasty. Kirban's salesmen began by ripping the price tags off the *Zico* packs rendering them unsellable, and given the chance would take the competition off the shelves altogether and throw it in the storeroom. Kirban, who had overcome childhood learning difficulties, was learning to get tough in the adult world of retailing.

Zico fought back by selling their product at crazy knock-down prices, leaving no space on the shelves for Kirban. Undaunted, Kirban added a degree of marketing sophistication to the campaign by encouraging his sales team to learn phrases in the languages of their customers who represented a variety of ethnic groups. But Kirban played dirty too by placing cartons of *Zico* next to sleeping vagrants and sending a photo to Rampolla, who retaliated by handing out free cartons of *Zico* on the doorstep of *Vita Coco's* head office. The water war was reaching boiling point. But Kirban and *Vita Coco* both came badly unstuck when they over-egged the properties of coconut water in their ads claiming, amongst other things, that their product could prevent kidney stones forming and improve virility. When a class action alleging the product contained considerably less sodium, potassium and magnesium than stated, and did not hydrate more effectively than other sports drinks, *Vita Coco* was taken to court. It changed its labelling and settled for a fine of US $10 million.

The company shrugged off the court action describing the claims they had made as a harmless error. It was not so easy, however, to shrug off the entry into the coconut water business of *Coca-Cola*, news of which cast a dark cloud over Kirban's head office in the Flatiron district of New York. The beverage giant took a stake in *Zico*, Kirban's main rival, and put the fear of God into the *Vita Coco* team. The coconut water wars were about to witness a battle of David and Goliath proportions – or so it seemed. But Kirban, who does his strategic thinking from the office hammock, refused to be cowered. Instead he went down the celebrity route, selling a stake in his business to a group of A-listers including Demi Moore, Spike Lee and Madonna. The singer Rihanna had already appeared on advertising posters. The celebrity endorsement shifted sales up a gear while *Coca-Cola*, who had paid US $8 million for their stake in *Zico*, failed to lift sales to the levels the industry – and Kirban – had expected. Having secured the business at home, Kirban turned to Europe and the Middle East, basing his international operation in London. His product was soon the market leader in the UK. By the beginning of 2017 worldwide sales were touching US $1 billion in a global market worth about US $2.2 billion.

The water from young green coconuts has become the fastest growing beverage the world has seen, and as market leader, *Vita Coco* can take much of the credit. At the latest count in 2016 there were forty different brands of coconut water on sale in the UK worth some £100 million in sales annually – twenty times the value of sales just four years earlier. The world market has passed the US $2 billion mark. *Vita Coco* remains way ahead of its rivals, and rumours of takeovers float around the industry. The company has diversified to include other coconut products in their portfolio, adding their own brand of coconut oil to an already crowded market. But sales of coconut water in the UK took a knock in 2018. *Vita Coco* continued to fare better than its rivals, but industry watchers were left wondering whether the growth over recent years was beginning to level off.

Coconut oil, on the other hand, produced by compressing the copra, has enjoyed a chequered history amongst nutritionists and health professionals and continues to be the subject of an ongoing debate about its benefits and dangers. Coconuts contain significant amounts of fat, but unlike other nuts, they provide fat that is mostly in the form of saturated medium chain fatty acids (MCFAs) and in particular one called lauric acid. (MCFAs are rapidly metabolised into energy in the liver.) It is thought that unlike other saturated fats, MCFAs are used up more efficiently by the body and are less likely to be stored as fat. This does not exempt them from contributing to heart disease – they are still fatty acids – but they have a different effect when compared to other saturated fats.

Lauric acid is converted in the body into a highly beneficial compound called monolaurin, an antiviral and antibacterial that, in laboratory experiments, has been shown to destroy a wide variety of disease-causing organisms. We can also more easily digest medium-chain triglycerides and convert them to energy. It is therefore now thought by some that consumption of coconut milk may help protect the body from infections and viruses. But, and it is a big 'but', the oil and milk of coconuts contain high volumes of saturated fatty acids (palmitic acid included) which tends to mitigate against the nut's health advantages. At least, that is what some experts believe. The fact is that ongoing research into fatty acids has left health professionals undecided about fatty acids and left the general public confused.

(The confusion over the health hazards of saturated fats is reflected in two cover stories in the American news magazine *Time.* On the magazine's cover of an edition in 1961 there was a picture of Ancel Keys, a dietary scientist, who claimed that saturated fats in the diet clogged arteries and caused heart disease. In a 2014 issue of the magazine, a cover story suggested scientists had been wrong all along and saturated fats did not cause heart disease after all.)

The fatty acid argument goes something like this. Cholesterol, first isolated from gallstones in 1784, has fascinated researchers from many areas of science and medicine. Thirteen Nobel Prizes have been awarded to scientists who devoted major parts of their careers to cholesterol research … Cholesterol is produced by the liver and helps to give cells their integrity by strengthening their membranes. It is the precursor of steroid hormones such as oestradiol and testosterone. But the liver produces all the cholesterol the body needs while additional and unwanted cholesterol comes as a result of fatty acids in foods – in some animal products and in a few plant products as well.

The link between excessive consumption of saturated fats and coronary heart disease is well established – at least it was until scientists discovered that cholesterol comes in two forms: HDL (high-density lipoprotein) and LDL (low-density lipoprotein), and doctors began to wonder whether saturated fats in our diet were as harmful as they once thought. When margarine became popular, manufacturers were seeking oil that was solid at room temperature and to achieve this used the process of hydrogenation. This led to the production of trans fats, which have been associated with an increased risk of heart disease and therefore deemed more dangerous than saturated fats. However, virgin coconut oil is solid (just) at room temperature so needs no hydrogenation to acquire a spreadable consistency.

The further good news for coconut lovers is that the predominant fatty acid in coconuts tends to mimic healthy unsaturated fats by boosting HDL, the so-called good cholesterol, which transports fats around the body in the bloodstream. These qualities may make coconut oil less bad than other saturated fats because HDL helps to round up and carry away its harmful cousin LDL. However, studies show that with the consumption of coconut oil, healthy HDL cholesterol levels appear to rise, but so too does unhealthy LDL cholesterol. This encourages some health professionals to claim that coconut oil loses out against healthy unsaturated fats, like those found in olive oil, which lower the bad stuff whilst increasing the good stuff too. New Zealand researchers examined the results of eight clinical trials and thirteen observational studies of coconut oil. The results: coconut oil raises LDL levels more than other vegetable oils, but not as much as butter does. The weight of the evidence, they concluded, suggests that if you eat polyunsaturated vegetable oils like soybean and canola instead of coconut oil, you will lower your risk of developing cardiovascular disease. Yet the popularity of coconut oil for cooking continues to grow. Top chefs remain ambivalent with some favouring olive as a cooking oil while others champion coconut milk and cream for flavouring and sauces. At home, jars of coconut oil find a place on kitchen shelves in ever increasing numbers. And for vegans, and those unable to tolerate lactose, coconut products provide a useful alternative to dairy products.

In the summer of 2018, coconut oil suffered a major setback when a leading epidemiologist described the oil as 'pure poison'. Professor Karin Michels of Harvard University's T.H. Chan school of public health was delivering a lecture in Frieburg, Germany – a lecture she called 'Coconut oil and other nutritional errors'. In it Professor Michels suggested that the oil was 'one of the worst things you can eat', basing her warning on the high proportion of saturated fat in the oil – more than 80 per cent – and the fat's proven association with raised levels of LDL cholesterol and the attendant risk of cardiovascular disease. The previous year, the American Heart Association, after looking at a large body of evidence on coconut oil, had delivered a clear warning: 'Because coconut oil increases LDL cholesterol, a cause of cardiovascular disease, and has no known offsetting favourable effects, we advise against the use of coconut oil.' It did not take long for a British cardiologist to accuse Professor Michels of bringing Harvard into disrepute, by making 'entirely false' claims. Dr Aseem Malhorta suggested her findings were not evidence based and should be retracted.

The British Heart Foundation took a more balanced view. One of the Foundation's senior dieticians warned against taking too much notice of speculative assertions about the oil. She told *The Guardian* newspaper that there had been speculation that some of the saturated fat present in coconut oil may be better for us than other saturated fats but 'so far there is not enough good-quality research to provide us with a definitive answer.' Using coconut oil occasionally was fine but, she advised, using unsaturated oils as an everyday choice was the sensible option.

As the health experts continue to disagree, leaving the public decidedly confused, the food pages of newspapers and magazines are full of coconut recipes. Coconut-seafood soup, tortilla chips made with coconut or coconut pork stew with coconut kale will satisfy those who like their coconut in savoury dishes. If you can't start the day without coconut there is almond coconut cluster granola, and if you like your coconut sweet there is coconut layer cake and cherry coconut ice cream sandwich. New Yorkers who beat a path to the Upper East Side can feast on coconut waffles with rum butter and fresh mango at Sarabeth's on Madison Avenue, or go for the hot stuff at Le Botaniste on Lexington which serves Tibetan Mama Coconut Curry. And if it is somewhere just to relax with a refreshing cup of tea, David's Tea on Third Avenue serves coconut oolong. For those looking for something stronger than a cup of tea, coconut beer is the answer – and there is a huge choice. Real ale enthusiasts speak highly of the Coconut Porter produced by the Maui Brewing Company on Hawaii. The Dangerous Man Brewing Company in Minneapolis makes a popular coconut stout. Mongozo Coconut, a pale ale brewed in Belgium, is becoming increasingly popular in northern Europe, while the Three Boys brewery in Christchurch, New Zealand does a coconut milk stout. British coconistas will find coconut yoghurt topped with honey-coated pecan pieces, toasted coconut shavings and cacao nibs at Pret a Manger, an iced coconut milk mocha macchiato at Starbucks and at EAT a mango and coconut chia pot.

Coconut is not to everyone's taste, however, but where the nut loses out on the palate, it gains ground on the skin. Soap still contains coconut oil as it did when Lever Brothers began making it in Victorian England. Skin creams and body lotions based on coconut oil crowd pharmacy shelves the world over. Gwyneth Paltrow, not content to merely 'pull' with coconut oil, slathers coconut oil over her body after her nightly bath. Lesser mortals use the expensive creams a touch more sparingly. Even so they contribute to a business which was worth billions of dollars in 2017 and showed every sign of expanding further. Eye-catching products range from coconut oil body polish and coconut oil-infused lipsticks ('keeps your pout looking healthy and sexy all day') to Burt's Bees Coconut Foot Cream, and an all-purpose coconut multitasking kit. *The Financial Times* suggested the coconut had become the hero product of the beauty industry. Tesco, Britain's largest supermarket chain, sells no fewer than 394 products containing coconut. The colossal success of coconut products owes much to some savvy marketing with assertions flying in the face of scientific research in a post-truth society.

6

DARK ARTS, BLACK MAGIC AND FAIR GAMES

By and large, the presence of the coconut on the world stage has been an entirely beneficial one. But there have been, and will continue to be, exceptions, some more serious than others. Puzzlement and a wry smile will have crossed the faces of *Guardian* readers when in September 2013 the paper quipped: 'Coconut detained in Maldives over vote-rigging claim.' (Some years earlier, readers of the *Guardian*'s sports pages had been treated to 'Queen in Brawl at Palace' after Crystal Palace striker Gerry Queen was sent off for fighting during a drawn game with Arsenal.)

The *Guardian*'s coconut story quoted the local Maldives news agency saying that police 'took the coconut into their possession around 7.05 a.m. after receiving a complaint about the suspicious fruit'. The mainly Sunni Muslim population of the Maldives blend myth and magic with their Islamic faith. The *Guardian* story explained that the offending coconut had been spotted on the Kaafu Atoll (population 2,000) outside a school being used as a polling station for the presidential election. Black magic was commonly used to dissuade people from voting, so the police moved in. The coconut was found to have a verse from the Koran inscribed in the shell, and the police summoned an expert in the dark art of black magic. After close examination, the nut was deemed safe and 'devoid of any harmful influence'. Voting at the school continued. Abdulla Yameen went on to win the presidency by a narrow margin, beating former president Mohamed Nasheed who was subsequently sentenced to a thirteen-year prison term for alleged terrorism offences. His legal representative, the human rights lawyer Amal Clooney, secured his release in 2016 to enable him to undergo hospital treatment in the UK.

While electoral black magic quite reasonably exercised the police in the Maldives, coconuts have come to the attention of law enforcement agencies elsewhere in circumstances a great deal more sinister. In May of 2016 US Customs and Border Patrol agents seized nearly 1,500lbs of marijuana at the Mexican border crossing at Pharr International Bridge in Texas. Sniffer dogs got excited when let loose on a trailer with a shipment of coconuts.

Agents found 2,486 separate packets of the drug concealed in the hollowed-out and carefully re-sealed nuts. The schedule one drug seized was valued at US $285,000. Cocaine worth £50,000 was found by UK border officers at London's Stansted Airport in 2011. The UK Border Agency staff became suspicious of a parcel carrying a customs declaration which claimed the contents were a variety of homemade non-perishable foods valued at £19. The parcel contained curry powders, black pepper and nine packets of dried coconut milk. But the packets of coconut milk each weighed considerably more than stated on the labels. Cocaine accounted for the extra weight.

In value terms, the Stansted seizure, commendable though it was, was modest set against a discovery made by customs officers in 2004. The 2004 drugs haul had its beginnings in the Caribbean when a self-confessed British smuggler called Andrew Pritchard claims he learned of a source of fake Cuban cigars in Guyana. There was also sandalwood at hand for some nice boxes, and coconuts, providing an innocent cover, were shipped regularly from Guyana to Spitalfields Market in London. Pritchard claims he and his accomplices, who included staff who worked at Spitalfields, began to hatch a plan with local Guyanan contacts. Sourcing the cigars would be straightforward, so too would be the making of boxes. And a container full of coconuts would be an ideal way of moving the contraband, especially since a member of his gang at Spitalfields could supervise the unloading without raising suspicion. There was one problem: coconuts are round and the boxes of cigars would be oblong. But Pritchard knew about container lorries: he had used them to smuggle cannabis from Jamaica. The containers that transported coconuts were refrigerated and the large refrigeration units offered an ideal hiding place. All this according to Mr Pritchard.

Satisfied that he could make the logistics work, Pritchard began to add the finishing touches to his operation. He says he checked on the price he could expect for the cigars, and told his people in Guyana to give the green light for their manufacture. A trusted courier was given bundles of cash for the contact in Guyana and was told to make sure she came back with the registration number of the container chosen for the job and a detailed account of how it was to be packed.

At this point Pritchard claims in his book *Urban Smuggler* that he was introduced to an ex-SAS soldier who had a brother working in Customs at Tilbury on the X-ray machines. The brother and his mates wanted to do business. For a fee they could ensure an identified container would be held under their control and put through the X-ray machine when it was switched off. It would get a clearance certificate and sent on its way. On 23 October 2004 Pritchard claims that 5,000 boxes of cigars left Guyana hidden amongst coconuts on a freighter bound for Tilbury. Well-schooled in the dark arts, Pritchard's accomplices used public phone boxes and a code to pass the container's number back to the UK whence it was passed on to the friendly customs team at the docks. Pritchard says his container was unloaded en route in Jamaica and sat on the quayside for a month. What Pritchard did not know was that by now it was the subject of a surveillance and intelligence operation run by Her Majesty's Customs Investigations Unit. The team had been listening to a number of interesting phone conversations between some known villains and had reason to believe the container of coconuts was concealing a very large quantity, not of cigars, but of cocaine. The unit did not inform customs officers at Tilbury about the operation.

With the help of foreign liaison officers, the container was tracked to Tilbury where it arrived on 2 December. But instead of taking the normal route through the customs sheds, it was diverted by the investigating team to a warehouse on the other side of the docks. Inside the container the customs officials found, as they expected, pallet upon pallet of coconuts. As each one was removed, sample nuts were smashed on the floor. But they revealed nothing. Given the quantity of cocaine they were expecting, the empty coconuts were beginning to sow doubts about the intelligence.

But then a pallet was exposed that did not look right. The sacks were the same but it was the bulges – not round this time but angular – that had everyone, by now ankle deep in coconut shells, stop in their tracks. Carefully and holding his breath, one of the team opened the sack. And there it was. Blocks of cocaine, enough to satisfy the habits of tens of thousands of addicts. At a first estimate the street value of the find was put at £100 million, making it the biggest drugs seizure ever in the UK. (The value was revised down later.)

Inside the container there was relief and some congratulatory exchanges. The sacks and the blocks of cocaine were photographed and fingerprinted. Blocks of wood cut to the same size as the blocks of cocaine were exchanged for the drugs, the sacks were sewn up again. The container was closed and sealed, united with its cab and sent on its way to Spitalfields market. There were eyes on the ground and in the air following its every mile. It was now 6 December and customs officers had laid their trap. It was not yet dawn and the officers mingling at the market were feeling the cold: others, smoking nervously, waited in the warmth of unmarked cars and vans. Hidden cameras were in place to record the unloading. Pritchard was there in a sporty Mercedes (he had borrowed it from his girlfriend at the last minute when his own car would not start) when the lorry carrying the container arrived. As soon as the unloading got under way the customs team pounced. Several officers came for Pritchard who claims the windscreen of his girlfriend's car was smashed as he was dragged out, thrown on the ground and handcuffed. Five other men were arrested along with Pritchard and all subsequently charged with offences connected with smuggling class A drugs.

The trial of the six took place almost a year later. Pritchard maintained throughout that he had been expecting cigars not drugs, and counsel for the prosecution failed to convince enough members of the jury otherwise. At the retrial, the jurors again failed to reach a verdict. After seventeen months on remand, Pritchard was a free man. A huge quantity of drugs had failed to reach the streets, but no one was paying the price for smuggling them into the country.

Nine years later, on a crisp November day in 2013, another intelligence-led drugs operation – this time in the hands of the Metropolitan Police Organised Crime Command – closed in on a gang operating from Leigh-on-Sea in Essex. A vehicle police had been tracking since early morning was ordered to pull over on the A13 just south of Dagenham. It failed to respond and attempted to force the police vehicle off the road. The passenger in the target vehicle was throwing out mobile phones as the chase ensued. With other police vehicles now in pursuit, the car was eventually brought to a halt and the two occupants arrested. In the boot of the car, police found not coconuts but carrier bags, from a Dutch supermarket, stuffed full of cocaine valued at around £1 million. The driver of the car was James Chrysostomou, a British Greek Cypriot. His passenger was Andrew Pritchard. Both men were found guilty of possessing class A drugs with intent to deal. Pritchard is serving a fifteen-year prison sentence, Chrysostomou sixteen years.

Cocaine is a dangerous drug and is at the root of much violent and sometimes deadly crime. But taken sparingly it rarely kills its user. Coconuts, on the other hand, can be outright killers. Legend has it that in 1777 King Tetui of Mangaia in the Cook Islands lost one of his concubines when a coconut fell on her head, killing her outright and leaving him deflated. More recent history records a surprising number of fatal accidents due to coconuts. In January 1943, a US marine was killed in his sleep when struck in the head by a falling coconut near Henderson Field, the US air base in the Solomon Islands. This unfortunate death may well have prompted Britain's Ministry of Defence to refine its warnings to members of the Queen's navy. The *Admiralty Manual of Seamanship* (Volume 2 1967) states in its survival section: 'Do not sleep under a coconut tree as a falling coconut may cause fatal injury.'

A mourner was killed by a falling coconut while attending a funeral in southern Sri Lanka. In Kota Baru Malaysia, Mat Hussin Sulaiman,76, the owner of a coconut plantation was killed when the monkey he used to do his picking hurled down a coconut, splitting his owner's skull open. Elsewhere in Malyasia, 6-month-old Nurul Emilia Zulaika Nasaruddin died after a coconut fell into her crib, landing on her while she was asleep. In August 2010, a 69-year-old man was killed by a coconut that fell out of a 39ft palm tree as he sat in a rocking chair outside his home in Melgar, Colombia. And a 40-year-old line manager at a margarine factory in the Ukrainian capital Kiev drowned when he fell into a vat of coconut oil.

Mindful of the deadly potential of falling nuts, the Indian government took the precaution in 2010 of removing coconuts from the trees at Mumbai's Gandhi Museum 'for fear that a nut would descend on to the head of President Obama'. When the president's visit to the city passed without incident, one newspaper observed: 'Thanks to Indian officials … Obama's recent visit to Mumbai was devoid of coconut trauma.'

But there was one occasion when the coconut palm could claim some credit amidst all the mayhem caused by its nuts. Kutubdia is a low-lying island in the Bay of Bengal off the coast of Bangladesh. It is subject to flooding leaving its people helpless in the eyes of storms and cyclones. In one such cyclone an islander lost six family members but saved a seventh, his son, by tying him to a coconut tree.

One man who has made it his life's work to investigate the hazards associated with specific environments is Dr Peter Barss, a Canadian public health physician. Dr Barss spent seven years running a remote hospital in Papua New Guinea where he made a study of trauma patients admitted to the hospital. A four-year review of those admissions to the hospital at Alotau, revealed that 2.5 per cent of such admissions were due to the patient being struck by falling coconuts. Since mature coconut palms may grow to a height of 35m and an unhusked coconut may weigh up to 4kg, blows to the head of a force exceeding 1 metric ton are possible. Of four patients with head injuries due to falling coconuts, two required brain surgery and two others died instantly in their village after being struck.

Barss published his findings in the *Journal of Trauma* and learnt to his amusement that he had won notoriety as one of 2001's 'Ig Nobel' prize winners. The prizes are awarded to the authors of the most oddball research papers in science by the editors of the *Annals of Improbable Research*, a bimonthly spoof of serious academic journals. 'The prizes are based on just one criteria,' explained the chair of the Ig Nobel judges,

> It's very simple. It's that you've done something that makes people laugh at first – and then think. Whatever it is, there's something about it that when people encounter it at first, their

> only possible reaction is to laugh. And then a week later, it's still rattling around in their heads and all they want to do is tell their friends about it. That's the quality we look for.

Barss told an interviewer that his prime interest was in the safety element of buildings but that safety for people in unaccustomed environments was a developing interest. He said he looked at how accidents, everyday accidents, occurred and suggested there was a tendency to neglect prevention. In Papua New Guinea it was the hill tribes who were most at risk from coconuts. Preventative advice was lacking. They were not used to coconuts in the hills, he said, and needed to be warned of the dangers when they came down to the coast.

Dr Barss would no doubt have been fulsome in his warnings to Charles Robinson. Dr Robinson was a botanist with a PhD from Columbia University. He took a job briefly as assistant curator at the herbarium in New York's Botanical Garden. Spreading his wings and travelling to the Philippines in 1908, he joined the staff of the Bureau of Science in Manila. From there he was sent to Ambon, an island in the Maluku archipelago, to collect species of the common and not so common plants peculiar to the islands.

In the absence of a Dr Barss to issue warnings about the hazards of particular environments, it fell to the islands' Resident (local administrator) Mr Raedt Oldenbarnevelt, to advise Robinson not to venture out in the rural areas alone, not least because his command of Malay was so poor. But the young Dr Robinson had the impetuosity of youth. On 3 December 1913 he set out alone on what to him was a routine plant collection exercise in the remote areas of the island. It seems Dr Robinson arrived at a small settlement deep in the island's interior and paused to take stock of his surroundings. A young lad who had climbed a palm to collect some coconuts saw the stranger and became frightened. The boy forgot all about his coconuts and hurried home to report the stranger's presence who, he said, had been following him. At the settlement a woman gave Robinson a glass of water, giving him no cause to consider his life was in danger. However, statements made to investigators by the boy suggest that his villagers were in fact in considerable fear of Dr Robinson, mainly because of rumours about headhunting that were doing the rounds of the islands. Headhunting had previously been observed in some parts of Indonesia where it was known as *potong kapala* (to chop one's head off) and it seems likely that Dr Robinson was mistaken for one such hunter.

Believing this to be the case, the headman of the settlement, armed with an axe, followed Robinson as he left the settlement. The headman apparently told his fellow villagers that he was going to track the 'dangerous' European who was intent on cutting their heads off and kill him before he killed them. Which is what the village headman did with the help of very violent accomplices. They wrapped Robinson's mutilated body in coconut leaves, weighted it with stones and rocks and tossed it into the sea. Reported missing six days after he set out, his death came as a shock to the islanders who had got to know the 'flower doctor' and treated him with respect and affection.

Looking for explanations for the pointless murder that reflected so badly on the island, it was pointed out that the word for head *kepala* sounded very like the Malay word for coconut *kelapa*. Could the gentle Dr Robinson with his poor command of the language mistakenly have asked if he could cut off the young frightened boy's head? It was one possibility. According to the children of Ambon, who regularly brought him plant specimens, he was always kind and friendly and quite incapable of causing harm to anyone. One Ambon resident, writing to the Governor General of the Dutch Indies, explained that Dr Robinson 'had taken a great liking to the population as they were always very kind and accommodating towards him on his many excursions through the interior of Ambon … Although I myself frequently advised him not to go out alone because he spoke Malay so poorly.' No one paid the price for Dr Robinson's murder. To commemorate his life a number of plants were subsequently named in his honour.

Coir is the fibre formed from the coconut husk found between the nut's shell and outer skin. The husk is thick and dense enough to provide protection for the seed when the nut falls to the ground. Spun into yarn it can be woven into matting as well as used by sailors for their ropes and rigging. In south Asia, ropemaking, which had begun as a cottage industry centred on Kerala in southern India, blossomed into a business on an industrial scale. India began making and exporting ropes and hawsers – the largest hawser being 24in in circumference and designed as a towing rope for tugs. For this, coir was thought to be ideal: it was light and it floated. But even the thickest coir ropes were proving less robust than expected. As ships got bigger and the tension on the ropes grew, doubts surfaced about coir's strength. Ropemakers responded by increasing the diameter of their ropes, but the extra width made it difficult to handle in all but a few specific situations. And the hangman was already making his noose not from coir but from hemp.

Disaster finally struck, not in the Arabian Sea off the southwest coast of India, nor off the Philippines in the South China Sea, but in the Irish Sea off the northwest coast of England. The *Primrose Hill* was a four-masted barque, square rigged, with a hull of iron that ran 300ft from bow to stern. It was built at Liverpool in 1886 with a registered tonnage of 2,332.56 tons. It was equipped with two lifeboats, a pinnace (a launch), a gig and a dinghy. On 23 December 1900, with a general cargo and under the command of its master Joseph Wilson, an experienced 49-year-old ship's captain, the *Primrose Hill* left Liverpool docks bound for Vancouver. It anchored in the

Coir hawser. (Ji-Elle, CC SA 3.0 via Wikimedia Commons)

Mersey where the ship and her crew spent the night. The following morning, 24 December, she left the river under the guidance of a pilot, Mr Henry Roberts, and was towed by the screw tug *William Jolliffe,* a boat of 250-horse power carrying twelve hands, one lifeboat, and the necessary life buoys and life belts.

The hawser connecting the ship to its tug was 120 fathoms (720ft) of 16in coir rope shackled to about 25 fathoms (150ft) of steel hawser, the latter being made fast to the ship. By 2.00 p.m. the *Primrose Hill* and her tug were passing Holyhead, and the ship's master signalled to the master of the tug asking for his assessment of the weather. The crew of the tug described the wind as 'moderate'. Moderate it might have been at the time, but William Owen, the coxswain of the lifeboat stationed at Holyhead, was surprised to see the *Primrose Hill* pass, given what he judged to be a barometer reading that suggested the weather was likely to deteriorate. It did. The wind began to freshen during the afternoon and evening and to back to the south east. By 9.00 p.m. Bardsey Lighthouse was 11 miles to the south east with the wind increasing. Then,

The four-masted *Primrose Hill* which sank off Holyhead in 1900. (State Library of South Australia)

without warning, the wind flew into a squall from the south west, catching the *Primrose Hill* on the wrong tack and putting a sudden and unexpected pressure on the coir tow line between the ship and the tug. The rope ruptured about 12 fathoms astern of the tug, setting the ship adrift in the gathering storm. Captain Wilson summoned all hands on deck. They were not an experienced crew – six of his twelve apprentices had not even been to sea before and four of them were just 15 years old. The tug came up on her starboard side. Her captain, shouting above the noise of the wind and the waves, could do little to help: there was no chance, he said, of reconnecting the line again. It was left hanging over the bows of the vessel and dragging along the side of the hull, making the control of the vessel even more difficult.

As darkness fell, the faces of the crew were showing signs of anxiety, and in some cases, plain cold fear. But the night passed relatively quietly. By 8.00 a.m. there were four sails set and a second attempt to haul in the trailing tow rope proved successful. More sail was set but the ship was making little headway. Another squall caught two of the staysails (small triangular sails) and blew them away. By midday, the wind had reached gale force, the sea was turning nasty and the *Primrose Hill* began to founder. At 1.00 p.m. she was sighted by those in charge of the South Stack Telegraph Station, who sent a telegram to the coastguard officer at Holyhead asking that the same tug *William Joliffe* be despatched immediately to the ship's aid. The master of the *William Jolliffe* was informed of this telegram by the coxswain of the lifeboat but made no attempt to leave the harbour. The *Hannah Jolliffe*, a smaller boat, made an attempt to put to sea, but was unable to get past the breakwater.

At 1.50 p.m. the master of the SS *Hibernia*, a vessel belonging to the London and North-Western Railway Company, en route from Dublin to Holyhead, sighted the *Primrose Hill*, heading down the channel on the starboard tack. The wind had reached force eleven, a violent storm, with a very heavy sea. The master of the *Hibernia* steamed up on the weather side of the *Primrose Hill* about two cables (a quarter of a mile) distant. He made ready his lifeboats, but made no attempt to launch them, considering it was not safe to do so. The *Primrose Hill* was now flying a distress signal, and several urgent telegrams were sent from the telegraph station for the dispatch of the Holyhead lifeboat and a team with rocket apparatus. The lifeboat made three attempts to leave harbour, but was unable to get outside the breakwater. Those in charge of the rocket apparatus (volunteers who used rockets to fire lines to stricken ships) not only promptly responded to the call, but did all that was possible to render assistance. At 2.15 p.m. the *Primrose Hill*'s anchors were dropped, and the ship swung head to wind. An attempt was made to take in sail but without success, and in about five minutes both anchors were dragging, and the vessel at once began to drive towards the shore. At 2.45 p.m. she struck the rocks just to the north of Penrhos Point. Such was the violence of the sea that by 3.00 p.m., or in less than a quarter of an hour, the ship had broken into pieces. Only one member of the crew survived – Able Seaman Johan Petersen from Sweden. Petersen had been on the poop deck when they hit the rocks and, by some miracle, had been swept ashore where he was found by a farmer and his son.

The loss of the *Primrose Hill* and her crew of thirty-three was the subject of a Board of Trade enquiry held in the County Court at Liverpool in April 1901, three months after the disaster.

> The Court having carefully inquired into the circumstances attending the above-mentioned shipping casualty, finds, for the reasons stated in the Annex hereto, that the loss of the vessel was due to her not having sufficient sail set to carry her clear of the shore after the tow rope parted. The loss of life was due to the ship so rapidly breaking up after she struck the rocks.
>
> Dated this 10th day of April, 1901. Signed: W.J. Stewart Judge.

Coir ropes are no longer used at sea. Not only were they not strong enough, but the thickness necessary to give them any strength at all made them impracticable. Alternative natural fibres such as hemp and manila have also lost favour as synthetic fibres have continued to improve.

But coir (from *kayar* meaning rope in the Malayalam language of Kerala) still has its uses. Some sixty years before the fateful voyage of the *Primrose Hill* it was in evidence for the christening of Queen Victoria's first born in St George's Chapel at Windsor. Albert Edward, Prince of Wales, later King Edward VII, was christened on 25 January in 1842 – an event recorded in a fine painting by Sir George Hayter which shows the baby prince in the arms of the Archbishop of Canterbury. The oil painting hangs in the ballroom annex at Buckingham Palace. *The Times* noted that the floor of the hall in the chapel 'was covered first with matting made of the husk of the cocoa-nut [*sic*]', and records at the chapel show that coir matting continued to be used throughout the nineteenth century.

The news that royal feet had found safe passage across what would have been the slippery stone floor of St George's Chapel, provided a boost for the coir matting makers. One such business was based on the banks of a river just west of London. Early in the nineteenth century, a mill on the banks of the Hogsmill, a tributary of the River Thames in Kingston, Surrey had switched from grinding flour to converting coconut husk into fibre for mats and brushes. By 1850 Britain was importing 1.5 million nuts annually, and Middle Mill in Kingston had become a volume producer of coir matting. Nine years after the christening of the Prince of Wales, the Great Exhibition of 1851, showcasing the products born of Victorian innovation and technology, provided a further boost for this new form of floor covering. News of the matting travelled far. By 1864 New Zealand had its first railway and within a decade express trains were operating between Christchurch and Dunedin, a journey of 370km which took eleven hours. Passengers were offered first class travel at a 50 per cent premium. In the same carriage and separated from second class by a modest partition, first class passengers were offered 'Horsehair cushions, brass spittoons and coir floor mats. And the quality of one's travelling companions.'

Back home, the Kingston coir mat factory was to become the catalyst for one of Britain's best-loved traditional games. In the 1860s the annual fair at Kingston took place on the banks of the Hogsmill River next to Middle Mill that produced the coconut mats. The local paper, the *Surrey Comet*, had been launched a decade earlier by a committed Christian called Thomas Philpott. (Philpott had a printing and bookbinding business in nearby Surbiton and when asked to print a flyer with the words 'Prepare to meet thy God', experienced some kind of revelation. A friend at the time suggested 'the light of God's truth' had broken in upon his mind. Thus enlightened Philpott vowed to produce a newspaper that would 'expose the bad and promote the good'. Idealist editors beyond Kingston doubtless make the same vows but not necessarily from similar revelatory experiences.)

One of the good news stories to appear in the *Comet* was the delight of Kingston folk at their own local fair. As the paper reported on Saturday 16 November, 1867:

> The Fair, held for the first time in the Fairfield [Kingston-upon-Thames] was larger than has been known for years. For the small sum of one penny, you could have three throws with sticks with the prospect of getting a cocoa nut, a doll, a pencil case, or some other such useful article … Then for a penny you obtain the privilege of trying to throw a ball into a gaping mouth, which when done, would entitle you to receive a cocoa nut, and you were assured you could crack it and try it.

It seems likely that the coconut prizes were donated by the adjacent mill, and in time coconuts balanced on sticks became the target for balls instead of tossing the balls into the gaping mouth of a so-called *Aunt Sally.* The coconut had become both target and prize: they called the new game the coconut shy.

Funfairs have been a part of British culture since medieval times, or rather fairs have been; the fun came later. King John signed his agreement to a tradesman's fair in the Buckinghamshire town of Amersham, a small market town 28 miles north-west of London, well before he signed Magna Carta. (Funfairs were established much later in Victorian times.) There were three main types of fairs: 'Prescriptive Fairs' which were based on the principle of trading and were established by custom; 'Charter Fairs', which were granted and protected by Royal Charter and 'Mop Fairs' which developed mainly in agricultural regions for the hiring of labourers. (The Mop Fairs were followed a week later by the 'Runaway Mops' which gave employers a chance to reconsider their decision and re-hire if necessary.) Between 1199 and 1350 over 1,500 charters were issued granting the rights to hold markets or fairs. Boston in Lincolnshire, Winchester, Stamford and St Ives acquired royal charters to hold huge, extended events focusing on international

A Victorian fairground coconut shy.

markets. These were trade fairs with farmers dealing in sheep and cattle while stallholders sold sacks of wheat and barley, horseshoes, cooking utensils, herring and eels, meats and damp pepper, wine from Bordeaux at 4p a gallon and chickens at 2p a throw. By the seventeenth century coconuts began appearing at the larger fairs, traded by enterprising merchants who snapped up the exotic fruit as it arrived at the docks in London.

The transition of these fairs from trade to leisure happened gradually as a merchant class evolved and powerful international organisations began to control trade on a grand scale. By the sixteenth century the trade fairs that owed their existence to royal charters had outlived their usefulness. But the charters were never revoked, and enterprising showmen saw an opportunity to make money by providing street entertainment at locations where royal charters were in existence. To start with sideshows were the main attraction at funfairs. There were menageries with lions, tigers, wolves and ostriches. Waxworks, stands with freak shows, and wrestling tournaments were supplemented by stalls selling snacks and drinks. These were joined in the late 1800s by the coconut shy. These funfairs were mainly working class affairs that expanded into much grander occasions with basic rides like roundabouts and merry-go-rounds propelled by gangs of boys paid a pittance to flex their muscles. With the arrival of the steam engine, the rides became more ambitious, and as travelling funfairs filled the streets that once played host to tradesmen and sheep farmers, the sideshows too offered an ever expanding and imaginative range of distractions. The coconut shy soon became a staple of travelling funfairs (the term coming from the old English 'cockshy' meaning a target at which stones were thrown) while the coconut itself was becoming a must-have novelty at home.

The proprietor of a coconut shy gets a walk-on part in the 1897 H.G. Wells novel *The Invisible Man*, and William Treloar, who succeeded to his father's coconut fibre matting business in the city of London, wrote of the nut's ubiquitous presence in his 1884 book *The Prince of Palms*:

> ... in nearly every country fair and in almost all the open spaces round London at holiday seasons, the cocoa-nut (sic) plays so conspicuous a part that every child is acquainted with it, most children have eaten it, and large numbers have tasted the thin, rather insipid liquor that is the 'milk' in a very deteriorated condition.

Treloar who was to be knighted and serve as Lord Mayor of London, noted the coconut's increasing involvement in popular British culture:

> The origin of the now neglected game of 'Aunt Sally,' also an importation from the tropics, may be attributed to the cocoa-nut; and at any rate the cocoa-nut 'shy' has superseded it by providing not only for the amusement, but the cupidity of the patrons of 'three sticks a penny.' It has also nearly superseded

> the more ancient 'cock shies' where the prizes were pincushions, knives, toys, and painted tin snuff-boxes – just as these covetable articles took the place of the gingerbread and gilded fowls that in earlier days displaced the live cocks at which the brutal part of the population threw sticks on Shrove Tuesdays.

The throwing sticks were themselves displaced by wooden balls and the coconut became the target: you dislodged a coconut from its perch and it was yours. The shy was well established by the time war broke out in 1939, winning a place at the heart of British fairground culture, and becoming the symbol of a carefree Britain letting off steam amongst straw bales on balmy summer weekends.

The fairground shies were the stimulus for a light-hearted poem by a little-known writer called Bernard Shaw (no relation to George Bernard Shaw):

> Twenty coco nuts all in a row,
> Painted with faces of people I know.
> A Politician right at the back,
> He is no good; I would give him the sack.
> Then the woman from over the way,
> She is loud mouthed, with plenty to say.
> A Teacher from long road school,
> He is always calling someone a fool
> Then the Policeman that grins as he books my car,
> Now that is a man that will go very far.
> The hypocritical Vicar, Him a Godly man,
> Making a mess of the good Lord's plan.
> The Dictators some old some new,
> Making weird plans for me and you.
> I do not like the coconuts or their faces;
> I will blot them out to leave no traces.
> In place of them, I will put myself;
> See if you can knock me off that shelf.

George Orwell's *Homage to Catalonia*, recounting his time in Spain during the Civil War, recalls an incident at the executive building of the Partido Obrero de Unificacion Marxista, [POUM] the party to which he had signed up on his arrival in the country. He was on an upper floor with his commander and friend Georges Kopp, the Russian-born engineer who some believe was having an affair with Orwell's wife Eileen, when the sound of huge explosions drove both men down to the street. Just inside their doorway they found Shock Troopers hurling bombs down the pavement 'as though playing skittles', wrote Orwell. The bombs were exploding just 20 yards from where they stood and bullets were flying everywhere. Across the street behind the newspaper kiosk, he saw the head of an American he knew well 'sticking up, for all the world, like a coconut at a fair'.

Orwell clearly had a thing about coconuts. In *Keep the Aspidistra Flying* he has Gordon Comstock in his bookshop surveying the shelves of the literary giants. 'Shall we ever again get a writer worth reading?' Comstock asks himself. 'But Lawrence was all right,' he concedes, 'and Joyce even better before he went off his coconut.'

Coconuts are around in Orwell's first novel based on his years with the Indian Imperial Police in Burma (now Myanmar). He was just 19 when he signed up and spent five years somewhat uncomfortably imposing colonial rule on the natives. The novel *Burmese Days* has as its protagonist John Flory, a teak merchant in his mid-30s disillusioned by empire and tired of the expatriate community of which he had become a part. Flory is lonely, a state of affairs tempered by his pretty mistress Ma Hla May who, muses Flory, had the 'mingled scent of sandalwood, garlic, coconut oil and jasmine in her hair'. But the earthy scent was replaced by finer fragrances when the niece of the owner of the local timber yard comes to visit, and Ma Hla May is unceremoniously removed from the house – and with her the smell of coconut oil.

The book was some ten years in the writing and originally turned down by British publishers who feared descriptions of some of the characters might deem it libellous. It was published in the United States in 1934, and only later in the UK when Orwell gave assurances that none of his characters could be identified.

The coconut shy was the English letting their hair down, and towards the end of the Second World War it even found its way into a prisoner of war camp in occupied Poland. At Auschwitz, adjacent to the concentration camp, there was a camp designated by the German High Command as Auschwitz E715. In the summer of 1944 it held some 150 British prisoners many of whom were forced to work as slave labour at the nearby IG Farben Buna Werke chemical complex. With news of Allied victories reaching the camp, spirits were high. By August there was enough confidence in the Russian advance that a group of prisoners – those still able to summon enough energy – decided to have some fun and organise a gala. There would be singing, a small roundabout, sideshows, a coconut shy and a pantomime in the evening. The impromptu funfair was in full swing (how the men managed to collect enough coconuts remains a mystery) when the air raid siren interrupted the proceedings. The men made for the brick-built shelter, but as the steel doors closed, the shelter took a direct hit. None of the men escaped injury. Thirty-eight of them died. They had survived the war thus far only to be killed by their own bombs – and with the end of hostilities just months away.

In the years after the war, with funfairs offering cheap entertainment, the cries of the showmen became a part of the background to post-war community rebuilding and normalisation. And none more so than the calls which beckoned fairgoers to the coconut shy. The refrain caught the attention of Harold Box and his colleagues Desmond Cox and Lewis Ilda. The trio were song writers and the novelty song they created celebrating the coconut shy was to become a popular standard. 'I've Got A Lovely Bunch of Coconuts' was composed by the songwriting trio in 1944 under the pseudonym of Fred Heatherton, and, for a novelty song, it was to enjoy quite extraordinary popularity and success. By 1950 the song had been recorded by the Billy Cotton Band, Danny Kaye, and the Freddy Martin Orchestra who took it into the top ten in America with vocalist Merv Griffin. Mel Torme, for reasons best known to Mel Torme, recorded it in 1957. Winifred Atwell with her piano did a recording for Decca in 1958, followed by Russ Conway a year later who included the number in his *Songs To Sing in Your Bath,* a compilation of clean, family songs he recorded for the Columbia label.

They like a Saturday sing-along at Cambridge United Football Club. The club, currently in the fourth tier of the English league, have their ground at the city's Abbey Stadium. In one corner of the ground, the club announcer has his little hut with its tannoy system and a pile of records to play at the end of the game. In the announcer's chair on Saturday afternoons in the 1950s sat club stalwart Jack Morgan. Jack was not a connoisseur of popular music. But it happened that after one winning game the record that sat on top of his pile was the Billy Cotton version of *I've Got A Lovely Bunch of Coconuts*. The familiar song rang out across the ground as the crowds dispersed to celebrate the win in the local pubs. Players and fans, delighted with their home win, suggested that Jack play the same song when the team next won at home. Sixty years later Jack's successor still plays the song after a home win. (There were a couple of occasions when somebody slipped in Perry Como's *Magic Moments.*) It is not the original 78 vinyl – that sits in the club museum – but it is the original Billy Cotton version. As a communal anthem of triumph, it means as much to Cambridge fans as *You'll Never Walk Alone* does to fans at Liverpool.

However, with mechanised high-rides and digital games dominating funfairs, coconut shies are losing their appeal. And the health and safety culture of twenty-first-century Britain is only helping to dampen fair organisers' enthusiasm.

'The location of the coconut shy must be selected to reduce the likelihood of stray balls hitting other site users ... the balls should be counted out and counted in to prevent theft or inappropriate use,' says the London Borough of Havering in its advice to schools. Bexley Borough Council warns: ' ... appropriate safety netting is positioned around the shy. This should protect against even the worst aimed shot!' And the council at Luton in Bedfordshire lists, in a twenty-page risk assessment document for fetes and fairs, two likely trouble spots: 'injuries caused by stray balls from a coconut shy' and 'someone accidentally eating a fire-lighter from the bar-b-q.' Health and Safety at its very best.

7

COCONUTS AND THE ARTS

It is one of the great photographic clichés of modern times. A palm tree leans lazily across a virgin beach as the digitally enhanced blue waters of the ocean lap the sand where the tree's fronds cast their shadows. The picture has become the visual shorthand for barefoot hedonism with a thousand travel brochures and as many websites using the palm to lure holidaymakers on packages to paradise. So firmly has the travel trade lodged the palm tree in the human consciousness as the byword for glamour and sophistication, that artificial trees are in huge demand as decoration for hotel lobbies, shopping malls, hospital atriums and in parks where real palm trees would not have a chance of surviving. Factories in China turn out the fakes in their thousands while British companies do classy bespoke trees for homeowners with tropical pretentions. Suppliers vie for space on the web. Wangyang Industries based in Guangdong offers a '6 metre Everygreen [*sic*] fake palm tree' for US $1,350. There is a choice of either a wooden trunk or one made from fibreglass. They have a lifespan of fifty years. Natural preserved leaves which have a lifespan of three years can be replaced at any time. The tree is guaranteed to be windproof, waterproof, ultraviolet-proof and snow-proof, and the finish makes it easy to clean. A British-based online supplier of fake trees, fake hedges, fake hanging baskets, and everything else fake for the reluctant gardener, does a fake coconut palm tree complete with fake coconuts.

Given the natural aesthetics of the real trees, painters have shown surprisingly little enthusiasm for setting their easels before the palm – with a few notable exceptions. Paul Gauguin, the French post-impressionist left Paris for Tahiti in search of the simple, primitive life in 1891, almost exactly a century after William Bligh had set sail on his own ill-fated South Seas mission. Gauguin had fallen out of love with France, his Danish wife and his five children, all of whom he abandoned. His paintings were not selling and he was destitute. In Tahiti he sought peace and solace, intending to paint illustrations for Pierre Loti's popular autobiographical novel *The Marriage of Loti*. But his eye was taken, as Loti's was, more by the beauty of the Polynesian women than by the beauty of the natural surroundings. He took teenage lovers – the youngest was just thirteen years old – and spread syphilis across the island. However, one painting did strongly feature the coconut palms. His *Thatched Hut Under Palm Trees* bursts with colour – and sexual promise. He nicknamed the hut *La Maison du Jouir* (The House of Orgasm). The painting is in the Musee d'Orsay in Paris. His other Tahitian works did include coconut palms but it was the Polynesian women who became the focus of his painting – and of his amoral life on the island. After two years on the island he returned to France expecting a welcome fitting his celebrity, and a resurgence in the popularity of his work. He got neither. He went back to the Polynesian islands expecting to find the paradise implanted in his mind. But the idyllic life eluded him.

Buddhist monks in Thailand pour purifying coconut water on the body of a woman prior to cremation. (Courtesy: Allen Hale World Photography)

Bligh and his loyal followers are cast adrift from the *Bounty*. (Robert Dodd, 1790)

Thatched Hut Under Palm Tree. (Paul Gauguin, Tahiti, 1896/97)

Left: A swastika, a Vedic symbol ensuring prosperity, is added to a coconut at a Jain wedding. (Sanjay Gohil Photography)

Poster for Gabriel Mascaro's film *August Winds.* (Courtesy: Desvia Producoes)

An early advertisement for Lever Bros Sunlight soap, drawn by John White and based on a painting by G.D. Leslie RA.

Weeping Coconuts by Frida Kahlo, 1951. Property of Bernard and Edith Lewin, currently on loan to the Los Angeles County Museum. (© Banco de Mexico Rivera Frida Kahlo Museums Trust, Mexico, D.F./ DACS 2018)

Michelangelo Pistoletto's *Doormats*. Property of Tate Modern. (© Michelangelo Pistoletto; Courtesy of the artist, Luhring Augustine, New York, and Galleria Christian Stein, Milan)

A seventeenth-century drinking cup in the form of a falcon, based on a coconut shell, by Samuel and Hans Kossborer. Feathers are carved into the coconut shell, and the silver hinged wings open when the cup is tipped. A bloodstone amulet engraved on the stomach of the bird was thought to guard against the drinker being poisoned. (The Rosalinde and Arthur Gilbert Collection on loan to the Victoria and Albert Museum)

The Holzschuher coconut goblet by Peter Flotner and Melchior Baier, Nuremberg 1535. (The German National Museum, Nuremberg)

A coconut is passed between bride and groom at a Hindu wedding. (Courtesy: Stephen Maloman Studios)

Gassed, John Singer Sargent, 1918.

Imelda Marcos's Coconut Palace, Manila.

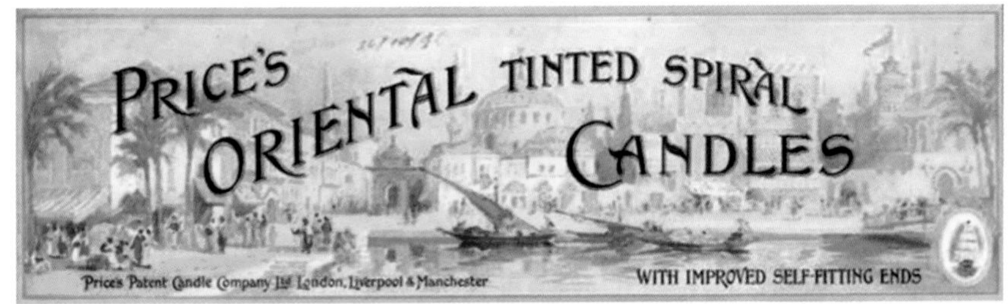

An advertisement for Price's candles.

Lever Bros Port Sunlight soap factory and staff housing on Merseyside at the beginning of the twentieth century. (Unilever archives)

Noble Woman with Black Slave, a 1783 painting by the Ecuadorian artist Vicente Albán featuring local fruits including coconuts. In paintings of this period a black slave conveyed a sense of status.

A Thai version of the Nasqareh with a coconut shell base. The percussion instrument has its origins in the Middle East where the instrument has a clay pot for a base. Various animal skins can be stretched across the top. (CC SA 4.0 via Wikipedia Commons)

A 1950s advertisement for the Mars *Bounty*.

A Hindu bride with a finely decorated coconut featuring Ganesh, an elephant's head on a human body, god of success and wealth and destroyer of obstacles.

The Coconut Monk's floating pagoda in the Mekong River, Vietnam. (Cserbell CC SA 4.0 via Wikimedia Commons)

Collecting coconuts in the Philippines. (Reuters)

Coconut rugby (*yubi lakpi*) in the north of India.

A nineteenth-century carved and painted coconut shell from New Georgia in the Solomon Islands. The shell contained a dark paste made from ground leaves which was used as a teeth blackener. Pitt Rivers Museum University of Oxford. Donated by HBT Somerville in 1895. (1895. 22. 103)

The minarets of a mosque climb above coconut palms in Kerala, southern India. (© The author)

The 50-rupee bank note issued by the Central Bank of the Seychelles.

He became depressed and bitter, and finally died in the islands that had once held such promise. (See p.3 of colour section.)

The Caribbean painter Francisco Oller, Gauguin's elder by fifteen years, did much to develop modern art in his native Puerto Rico. He began his art studies when he was eleven and later spent time in both Madrid and Paris where, like Gauguin, he spent time with Camille Pissarro who nurtured his journey into impressionism. Oller took inspiration from his tropical surroundings at home in Puerto Rico, painting landscapes and still life featuring local fruits. His *Still Life with Coconuts* features young green coconuts and was completed in 1893. Exhibited extensively throughout the United States, the painting is currently in a private collection in New Jersey. A large number of his other works were lost after his death in 1917 when he was 84, and none have so far been retrieved.

Weeping Coconuts is one of Frida Kahlo's later and least known works, and it reflects an unfulfilled and pain-ridden life. Kahlo was born in 1907 in a suburb of Mexico City, the daughter of a photographer. She contracted polio when she was 6, and at the age of 18 was caught up in a terrible traffic accident when the wooden bus she was riding was rammed by a trolley bus. Her spine and pelvis were both broken in three places, her right leg in eleven places. In her hospital bed, she began to paint with a mirror placed above the easel so she could paint herself. *The Broken Column* was a self-portrait wearing a polio corset and depicting her horribly broken spine. Her recovery was only partial and she could no longer contemplate her chosen career in medicine and she was in pain most of her life. There was emotional pain too. Her husband, the muralist Diego Rivera, was unfaithful and had an affair with her sister. Frida suffered a miscarriage and doctors, fearing her damaged pelvis was too weak, advised against continuing with two further pregnancies. Kahlo and Rivera divorced. Kahlo was bisexual and her affairs with women included one with the singer and dancer Josephine Baker. Amongst her male lovers was the Russian Marxist revolutionary Leon Trotsky who lived in the

Kahlo family home after Mexico granted the exiled Russian political asylum. Despite both of them indulging in numerous affairs, she and Rivera remained friends, were soon reconciled and remarried in a simple ceremony towards the end of 1940.

Kahlo's preoccupation with self-portraits led one critic to describe her recently as the 'mother of the selfie'. A 1929 self-portrait sold in 2000 for US $5.1 million, and her self-portrait with a monkey and a parrot sold in 2013 for US $3.2 million. She explained once that she painted self-portraits because she was so often alone and that she was the person she knew best. By her early 40s, Kahlo was relying on drugs and alcohol to manage the pain which was preventing her from painting with the precision she demanded of herself. (She concealed her prosthetic leg under extravagant, spectacular skirts and dresses.) Increasingly she turned to still life and in 1951, three years before she died, she produced *Weeping Coconuts*, a small 9in x 12in work in oil on Masonite (a type of hardboard) in which one of two nuts produces tears – a clear reflection of her pain. She created the picture for Elena Boder, a physician friend. A flag, lodged in a fruit in the bottom left of the picture, carried the inscription 'For Elena Boder. Painted with great affection. Frida Kahlo.' Boder, however, did not like the picture and sent it back. Kahlo, disappointed but resilient, painted over 'for Elena Boder' and sold the picture to Bernard Lewin, a collector of Latin American art. Kahlo died three years later in 1954 at the age of 47. And in common with so many artists, has enjoyed considerably more international recognition in death than she ever did during her short life. Staging a major exhibition of her work in 2005, London's Tate Modern tellingly said of Kahlo: 'She is now regarded as one of the most significant artists of the twentieth century.' What has surprised many is the lack of social comment in her work. She was a communist, a feminist, and overtly political but rarely used her art as a means of political expression. (Whether British Prime Minister Theresa May intended to make a political statement by wearing a Frida Khalo bracelet at the 2017 Conservative Party Conference was the subject of much speculation.) *Weeping Coconuts* is now on loan to the Los Angeles County Museum of Art. (See p.6 of colour section.)

In contrast to Kahlo's work, the paintings of Clement Siatous are historical documents much concerned with coconuts and full of political intent. If they were not so, critics would likely dismiss them as kitsch. Clement Siatous was born in 1947 on Peros Banhos, a tiny atoll in the Chagos Islands, an archipelago in the Indian Ocean some 800 miles from the Maldives. When the family moved to the larger island of Diego Garcia, Clement, now in his early 20s, became seriously ill and was evacuated to Mauritius for treatment. He recovered well and was about to go home when the British authorities closed his island preventing his return. The Cold War was exercising the British and American defence establishments and Diego Garcia had been sold to the Americans as a military base. While Clement was prevented from returning, those still on Diego Garcia were forcibly evacuated. Disingenuously the British government maintained the islanders never really existed and, if they did, they would not be indigenous but migrant workers who could be returned to Mauritius or the Seychelles.

Saddened, frustrated and angry at being marooned on Mauritius, Clement Siatous started painting as a way of expressing his inner turmoil. The islands in the archipelago had established a flourishing trade in coconut products, exporting coconut oil and dried copra, and many of the pictures Siatous produced while in exile featured the coconut palm in one form or another. In one a smiling woman carries a huge basket of nuts on her head and in another a crab climbs a palm tree. Men traditionally harvest coconuts, but in one large canvas completed in 2015, two women dressed in blue and touting coconuts take centre stage. His pictures become a narrative describing a sorry tale of a community uprooted, a life lost on islands where resources had been plentiful. In exile in Mauritius, the Seychelles, and later in the UK (there is a community of Chagos islanders in Crawley near Gatwick Airport where they were dumped in the late 1960s and early 1970s) life was tough. (In March 2019 The United Nations ruled that Britain must 'bring to an end its administration of the Chagos Archipelago.')

Siatous called the first solo exhibition of his work, in New York in 2015, *Sagren*, the creole word for regret. With the show, the cause of the exiled islanders was once again brought sharply into focus. The British Labour leader Jeremy Corbyn, who has backed the campaign to allow the Chagossians to return home, accused the government of failing to deliver justice to the islanders who had been 'abominably treated and brutally removed from their homes'. In confirming that there would be no re-settlement, a British Foreign Office minister told the British parliament in 2017 that the manner in which the people of the Chagos Islands had been removed 'was wrong and we look back with deep regret'. The paintings of Clement Siatous will be a reminder for his fellow islanders of a simple but happy life amongst the coconut plantations of their coral islands. For the rest of us they are a reminder that in an increasingly dangerous world, realpolitik can play havoc with people's lives – and in unexpected ways.

Politics is not infrequently on show in the works of artists given space at London's Tate Modern. Coconuts are a little rarer. It took an Italian to bring both politics and coconuts together in a single work. The artist, Michelangelo Pistoletto, believes art's role in society is to change the status quo and especially to encourage sustainability. At first sight any political message would be hard to discern in a pile of doormats. But his doormats are made of sustainable coconut fibre. They are set on a rubber base and were acquired by the Tate in 2006 – one of his five pieces the gallery has in its collection. The piece consists of twenty mats on top of each other to form a shape that reflects an angular egg timer. Some questioned whether the piece was art, just as two decades earlier many were struggling to see the art in works by the likes of Damien Hirst and Tracey Emin. If the aesthetics were missing, the message carried in the sustainable coconut fibre of the mats was clear enough. (See p.6 of colour section.)

Born in 1933 in Biella, a city in Piedmont rich in Romanesque and Renaissance architecture, Pistoletto was introduced to art in his father's studio where Pistoletto senior restored damaged paintings. Like Kahlo in Mexico, the young man produced large numbers of self-portraits until in his mid-30s when he began transposing everyday items into works of high art. With Giovanni Anselmo, Giuseppe Penone and Gilberto Zorio, Pistoletto became associated with an avant-garde movement referred to as *Arte Povera* (Poor Art). Using everyday articles in unexpected ways, he called on people to impose their identities on the variety of objects that surrounded them. The shape of his own collection of door-mats represents his outstretched arms and legs. Pistoletto, now in his 80s, spends his time between Turin and his Cittadellarte complex in Biella where under his inspiration, art meets politics, production and economics. He was awarded the Golden Lion for Lifetime Achievement at the 2003 Venice Biennale.

Like Pistoletto, Julian Charrière puts politics at the centre of his artistic creations. Born in the French speaking part of Switzerland and now based in Berlin, Charrière is a conceptual artist concerned with the relationship between art, technology and science. He spent six months on the Bikini Atoll, the site in the Marshall Islands (in the South Pacific between Hawaii and Australia) where the Americans tested twenty-three nuclear devices between 1946 and 1958. (A popular myth in the islands has a woman giving birth to the first coconut.) The Atoll is now safe for visitors although they must bring their food and water with them. However, the coconuts are still radioactive as their roots are embedded in what is still contaminated soil and groundwater. In his most recent exhibition Charrière pays tribute to the people of the Marshall Islands with his installation that includes radioactive coconuts piled on the floor. They are coconuts that Charrière himself collected and are now carefully wrapped in lead sheaths.

Resettlement of the atoll began in 1968 with US President Lyndon Johnson ordering all necessary assistance be given to the 540 islanders who wanted to return. But just ten years later, tests showed an unexplained but significant increase in levels of radioactive cesium, and the island was again evacuated. A handful of caretakers remain on the atoll, one of whom acts as the divemaster for a regular trickle of diving enthusiasts who report surprisingly healthy communities of coral and large schools of reef sharks.

Being invited to exhibit at the world's leading art galleries and/or catching the eye of established private collectors provides the seal of approval for an artist's work, while not necessarily guaranteeing mass exposure. Mass exposure is guaranteed when artists beat a path to the doors of the governors of central banks and the directors of national postal services. 723 million £10 notes are currently in circulation in the UK; 11.4 billion green backs (dollar bills) do the rounds in the United States. And they all bear an artist's work. Yet the designs on bank notes (the Chinese in the seventh century were the first to use notes) mostly pass unnoticed – unless they become controversial, as they did in Britain recently, when the very small number of women joining Her Majesty the Queen on UK banknotes became an issue. (Jane Austen has now joined the queen on the latest issue of £10 notes designed by the security printers De La Rue and brought into circulation in September 2017.)

The portrait of George Washington on the $1 bill is by Gilbert Stuart, considered by many to be one of America's great portraitists. Stuart painted the first six American presidents. He worked fast, eschewing preliminary sketches and left much of his work unfinished. The banknote portrait of Washington, commonly referred to as *The Athenaeum*, was one of the unfinished works. The head and shoulders of the president are complete (enough for an image on a stamp) but there is no torso, and much of the background is blank canvas. Stuart spent his formulative years in England and Scotland fleeing to Ireland when, short of money, he feared ending up in the debtors' prison. He never did get on top of his financial affairs, and when he died in Boston in 1828 he left his wife and children with massive debts.

One banknote issued by one of Her Majesty's colonies commanded uncommon attention and set in motion a hunt for the banknote's designer. The 50 rupee note issued in 1968 by the Central Bank of Seychelles carried a design which was, at first sight, pleasing but innocuous. It is a seascape with hills climbing from the shore in the background, and a two-masted brig under full sail in the foreground. The signature of the bank governor is clearly visible under the bowsprit. The queen's head, reproduced from the full-length portrait of the young Queen Elizabeth commissioned in 1955 by the Worshipful Company of Fishmongers from the Italian portrait artist Pietro Annigoni, is on the right within a conventional oval frame. To the right of the queen's head are two coconut palms. Glanced at as the note changed hands there was nothing exceptional about the palm trees. But examined closely, and by turning the note upright, it becomes clear that the fronds of the palm are arranged to spell SEX. It seems that by 1968 the Seychelles were agitating for independence and investigators at the time, having established the note's two artists were innocent of the prank, concluded that a rogue engraver at the south London printer Bradbury Wilkinson, sympathetic to the islanders' yearning for self-rule and intent on insulting the Crown, fiddled with the design. There were others who passed off the scarcely hidden word as a printing anomaly but their assessment lost credence when a second Seychellois banknote of the same period was examined closely. The 10 rupee note, with the same picture of the queen, features a rather splendid turtle. Under the turtle and deftly hidden in the coral is the word 'scum'. One printing anomaly perhaps, but two in the same period at the same company seems unlikely. No one ever owned up to the prank, and neither note was withdrawn. When the Seychelles eventually gained their independence in 1976, new notes were printed featuring a portrait of the first president

Sir James Mancham in place of the queen, and a lion fish in place of the turtle. Forty years later at an auction house in the west of England, a 50 rupee SEX note was sold for £336, 120 times its face value. (See p.16 of the colour section.)

Little troubled by banknotes featuring hidden words, the Seychelles government has continued to show off its coconuts on a series of stamps. (A few square centimetres of sticky paper with perforated edges gives an artist little scope for creativity subversive or otherwise.) But a series issued in 1980 features the coco-de-mer, a palm that produces huge double coconuts. The tree is extremely rare, found on Praslin, the Seychelle's second largest island. On the tree, the coconut is a giant green orb, but with the outer husk removed it resembles a well-formed woman's bottom. Tourists flock to see the coco-de-mer, partly because it is the biggest seed in the world – a true botanical curiosity – and partly because of its naturally erotic shape. In China, the copra (meat) of the nut is taken as an aphrodisiac. The Duke and Duchess of Cambridge were presented with a coco-de-mer while they were in the Seychelles on their honeymoon. The nuts fetch high prices and an export permit is needed to take them out of the country. What puzzles botanists is how a plant that grows in poor quality soil on just two islands produces record-breaking nuts that reach half a metre in diameter and can weigh around 25kg.

Pollination too remains a mystery. The trees themselves are clearly male and female. The female tree bears the nuts while the male trees grow enormous phallus-shaped catkins which have hundreds of tiny yellow flowers on the surface giving off a musky odour. Some researchers believe bees do the pollinating while others suspect local lizards are involved. But with the bottom-shaped nuts weighing up to 25 kilos neither the wind nor animals could affect the dispersal. A local legend says that during a full moon the male coco-de-mer trees walk around the forest in order to mate, tearing themselves from the ground and locking in passionate carnal embrace with the female trees.

To date the coconut designs on the banknotes of the Maldives have fallen foul neither of printing anomalies nor from subversive manipulation. The series of notes printed in the early 1980s by the same company that printed the notes for the Seychelles government, were considered to be some of the most beautiful in the history of banknote design. The 10 rufiyaa note is an unrestrained celebration of the coconut. A village scene, with huts in the background, has a turbaned woman by a tree beating coir from a coconut husk. The coconuts are buried in wet sand to soften them, before the coir is removed by beating the coconut. A woman to the right is creating a panel to be used for the wall of a hut by weaving coconut fronds with coconut fibres. A third woman in the middle distance is seated by a tub making coconut oil. The reverse side, common to every denomination note, features a bunch of green coconuts and a *Dhivehi Odi*, a *dhow* made of coconut timber. None of the Maldivian notes carry a promissory clause, but they are signed by the then president of the country and the governor of its central bank, Maumoon Abdul Gayoom. They are printed with two dates – 1 Muharram 1404 (from the Islamic Hijri calendar) and 7 October 1983. A new set of notes was introduced in 2015 designed by the local artist Abdullah Nashaath. The new 10 rufiyaa note is another monetary celebration of the coconut with a toddy tapper (one schooled in extracting the sap from the tree) dressed in a colourful sarong climbing a coconut palm. In the background a group of men and women play traditional drums as if encouraging the climber. The new notes still lack a promissory clause (there has never been a hint of the monetary authority not honouring the notes) but still carry the date from both the Gregorian calendar and the Muslim Hijri calendar – 2015 and 1436.

While the aesthetics of the palm tree have largely failed to seduce painters, the nut itself had the opposite effect on sculptors, silversmiths and goldsmiths who seized on the nut's potential with relish. The nuts were a rarity, at least to begin with, and they came from distant lands which added to the sense of the exotic. But before the artisans got hold of them, they were seized upon by healers. Those first coconuts to arrive in medieval northern Europe were wrapped in myth and credited with all manner of healing powers. Coconuts had already been associated with miracles and were displayed as rarities in Greek temples. They were found in reliquaries in medieval treasuries, and there were stories, too, of how seafarers facing shortages of both food and water had survived on coconuts alone – stories that found foundation in the lives of sailors centuries later. These reports by seamen in particular suggested to many that coconuts possessed medicinal qualities. With no scientific evidence whatsoever to support the idea, coconuts were suddenly a cure for all manner of illnesses. The coconuts that found their way to England and the ports of northern Europe in the fourteenth and fifteenth centuries came on ships from Venice, together with silks, sugars, spices and exotic pets like monkeys and parrots. And there was an alternative overland route that linked Venice with Augsburg, Nuremberg, Prague and Vienna via the Brenner Pass.

The 'medicinal' coconuts were having some success as placebos and the shells were being turned into drinking cups, especially in those towns and cities where woodworkers had established their crafts. The first carved coconuts, however, were brought home by navigators and explorers who would gather the nuts during their trips to the South Sea islands, and work on them during the long passages home in much the same way as fellow sailors would work on whales' teeth and bone to produce what we know as scrimshaw. Well-to-do families, eager to show off their wealth and their connections with distant lands, displayed them in 'cabinets de curiosités' and in patrician homes in Germany in *Wunderkabinetts*. The nuts left over from the curio cabinets and medicine chests gave the carvers and sculptors and silversmiths their chance. Decorated with silver or with pieces of enamel, the coconuts were considered as precious as jewellery. Over time, engravings became more and more sophisticated, and coconuts were finely carved with charming animated scenes, mythological characters, and personalities of the time. The silver came from Spanish America – or to be more precise from Potosi in what is now Bolivia, and later from mines in Mexico. For the craftsmen of sixteenth-century Europe, this Spanish silver was to trigger the blossoming of new-found creativity, one which would combine the abundance of silver with increasing numbers of otherwise unwanted coconut shells.

The production of fine goblets fashioned from coconuts and embellished with silver – and sometimes gold – became the signature of the precious metals craftsmen of Antwerp, Nuremberg and Augsburg. Nuremberg reached its creative zenith during the lifetime of Albrecht Dürer, himself born in Nuremberg and the leading light of the German Renaissance. Dürer's interest in depicting the natural world led to his collecting rare and exotic items, and to accepting gifts in exchange for portraits – gifts that included a tortoise shell, two dried fish and sixteen Indian coconuts.

Peter Flotner, the Nuremberg sculptor, had already earned himself a reputation for woodcarving when he embarked on his first coconuts. He was born in Thurgau in Switzerland and probably trained in Augsburg before moving in 1522 to Nuremberg where he took the oath of citizenship. He quickly stood out as an innovative sculptor and designer, and judging by his style, it is likely he spent time in Italy. One of his finest works was the so-called 'Holzschuher Goblet', an intricately carved coconut shell, resplendent with Italianate flourishes and completed around 1530 in collaboration with a German goldsmith called Melchior Baier. The piece is 17 inches in height with the coconut shell, carved by Flotner, forming the body of the goblet. (Flotner also made the models of figures worked in silver by Baier.) His carving in low relief represents the triumph of Bacchus, incorporating all the debauchery that comes with an excess of wine. Bacchus, naked and overweight, leads his procession on a cart drawn by a goat with the help of two naked men pushing from behind, while a third fills a pitcher held in Bacchus' outstretched hand. The coconut is divided into three panels by vertical silver bands, and in the next panel there is more drunken revelry and more still in the third section where a couple make love, and a drunk, who appears to have had his genitals removed by some offended viewer of the piece, is supported by two hapless women. And a satyr is being sick over one of the men pushing the cart. The base of the piece is composed of gilded silver. On top of the base comes a laurel wreath, and above that a landscape with boulders and tree stumps. From the centre of the landscape a stem climbs upwards with a vine of grapes and leaves twisted around it. A naked child (or cherub) stands next to the vine with feet apart, holding a shield with the Holzschuher coat of arms. Elsewhere a goat is mounting a ewe, causing a woman seated nearby to hide her eyes behind a corner of her shawl – although on closer inspection it is clear she is peeping over the top of the cloth, enjoying what's going on. To her left Baier has a pair of figures, a reclining bearded satyr and a woman holding a tankard in her lap while attempting to arouse her companion with strokes from the back of her free hand. On the lid the carved mining scenes are a clear reference to the mining side of the wealthy Holzschuher family although there is no evidence that the family commissioned the work. (It is possible that the canny Flotner included mining to flatter the family and encourage them to buy the goblet.) The lid is topped with two more figures in gilded silver – a naked man lying on a grassy bank with a satyr standing over him, legs well apart, pouring wine down his throat from a very full wine skin. The goblet was still with the patrician Holzschuher family in 1897: it is now in the German National Museum in Nuremberg. (See p.7 of colour section.)

In the first half of the sixteenth century Antwerp silverware combined with coconut shells was matching anything Nuremberg could produce from the nuts and silver gilt. A goblet in the form of an owl – the oldest known Antwerp piece made from coconut – with the nut forming the bird's body is considered a technical masterpiece, reflecting the development and wealth of the port of Antwerp, the arrival of exotic goods from distant shores and the high quality of local craftsmen. At the side of the silversmith's hallmark – a pelican and the date 1548–1549 – there is a little hand that reminds the viewer of the legend of Brabo who cut off the hand of Antigone the giant and threw it into the River Escaut. Although the artist is unknown, there seems little doubt that the piece came from those silver studios of Antwerp. There is another fine Antwerp goblet which has three scenes carved into the coconut shell based on prints by Hans Sebald Beham (1500–1550). The scenes are from the story of the Prodigal Son (Luke 15: 11–32). They show the Prodigal Son leaving his parental house, his life spent squandering his inheritance, and his return home. A silversmith then placed the coconut in a silver mounting and transformed it into a display goblet. (See p.7 of colour section.)

The Metropolitan Museum in New York has a coconut and silver gilt goblet dated 1524 by the Dutch craftsman Hans van Amsterdam. It stands 11in tall with carvings on the coconut representing heroic themes from the Old Testament: Lot and his daughters, Samson and the Lion, and David with Bathsheba. The nut is gloriously mounted in silver gilt and decorated with herm figures – sculptures with a head, no defined torso, a plain and usually a squared lower section on which male genitals may also be seen at the appropriate height. The form originated in Ancient Greece and was revived at the Renaissance in the form of term or herm figures. Latin inscriptions warn of the dangers of an excessive appreciation of wine. The Hermitage Museum in St Petersburg has a much later example of coconut craftsmanship, with an eighteenth-century goblet by an unknown Moscow artist who made carvings in the nut of the Imperial double eagle and a detailed representation of the badge of the Order of St George. And with enthusiasm for coconuts amongst Russia's craftsmen showing no sign of flagging, a nineteenth-century coconut tankard with silver gilt mounts, now held in a private collection, has finely worked portraits of Peter the Great, Catherine and their daughter Yelisaveta etched into the coconut. Yelisaveta was born before her parents were officially married and after her father died she staged a *coup d'etat* against her cousin Anna's supporters. She had many lovers but produced no children to take over her crown. She reigned as empress until her death in 1762.

It was probably in the workshops of the goldsmiths in Augsburg at the end of the sixteenth century, when local gold and silversmiths flourished under the patronage of the Imperial Court, that one very rare piece of coconut sculpture took shape. It is rare because the nut was a double nut, a coco-de-mer, from the Seychelles. In this case, only one half of the nut was used, giving the piece its distinctive shape compared to pieces fashioned from the regular coconut. It is embossed and chased with silver gilt. Given the opening in the top and an elaborate spout in the form of an animal's head, it was likely intended as a ewer or scent fountain. Its provenance is unclear until it reached the collection of Anselm Rothschild, the Austrian banker and member of the Vienna side of the Rothschild family. It remained in the family until it was bequeathed to the British Museum, where it arrived with a very fine silver gilt addition to the cap on the top depicting Jupiter astride his eagle.

British craftsmen soon followed in the footsteps of their European counterparts. In London's Science Museum there is a late seventeenth-century, silver-mounted coconut goblet decorated with three scenes in the life of a barber-surgeon. One shows a bloodletting scene, a common treatment for a number of illnesses and diseases. The other scenes show a customer waiting for a haircut and shave, and a patient with a bandage on his head who is also waiting to be seen. Although the practical links between the professions of barber and surgeon are long gone, the historical connection lives on in the red and white striped poles (the coloured stripes representing blood and bandages) which can still be found outside barbers' shops in industrial towns across Britain.

In modern times, carved or decorated coconuts have served as gifts for the great and the good. Queen Elizabeth received a painted coconut bowl from Belize in 1985 presented by the people of Dangriga in the south of the island. The artwork would not earn a place in Her Majesty's cabinet of curiosities (and would be given short shrift by the hanging judges at the Royal Academy) but the coconut resides quietly in Her Majesty's collection of gifts from the Commonwealth and makes an occasional appearance at events celebrating the diverse cultures of those nations that belong to the Commonwealth.

The decorated coconut presented to Barack Obama shortly after his inauguration in 2009 travelled to Washington by train from New Orleans wrapped up in an old Faberge eggbox. Taking it in turns to cradle the boxed nut on the journey were Charles Hamilton Jr and his wife Patricia Wade Hamilton. The Hamiltons were president and first lady of the celebrated New Orleans Zulu Social Aid and Pleasure Club. The club does indeed organise social aid and its members clearly get a great deal of pleasure from parading at Mardi Gras when they traditionally toss painted coconuts into the crowd from their floats. But Zulus they are not. They are, in the majority, African Americans who in previous years had blackened their faces and donned grass skirts at Mardi Gras and adopted, somewhat disingenuously, the Zulu name. In the 1960s, their name and their carnival costumes got them into trouble from civil rights activists. The protesters advertised in the local black community's newspaper the *Louisiana Weekly* in an effort to have the club boycotted:

> We, the Negroes of New Orleans, are in the midst of a fight for our rights and for a recognition of our human dignity which underlies those rights. Therefore, we resent and repudiate the Zulu Parade, in which Negroes are paid by white merchants

> to wander through the city drinking to excess, dressed as uncivilized savages and throwing coconuts like monkeys. This caricature does not represent us. Rather, it represents a warped picture against us. Therefore, we petition all citizens of New Orleans to boycott the Zulu Parade. If we want respect from others, we must first demand it from ourselves.

The club, with the support of the mayor and chief-of-police, refused to bend to pressure and continued to parade, but gave up painting their faces blacker than they already were. And they abandoned their grass skirts. However, they continued to toss the painted coconuts from their floats, which only brought more trouble. In 1987, the club was unable to renew its insurance coverage because of lawsuits stemming from coconut-related injuries amongst the crowd at the 1986 festivities. But once again the law was on their side. In a surprise move the following year, the state governor Edwin W. Edwards signed Louisiana State Bill SB188, the 'Coconut Bill', into law, removing liability from injuries resulting from coconuts and enabling the tradition of tossing coconuts into the crowd to resume.

The nut which the Hamiltons had taken to Washington had been decorated by schoolteacher Keith Eccles from Gretna, on the west bank of the Mississippi River, just east and across the river from uptown New Orleans. His design featured the face of a Zulu member on one side and a flag rippling over the White House, flanked by Zulu spears, on the other. But the path to the Oval Office had its obstacles. The White House secret service agents had not been warned in advance that an old egg box supposedly containing, of all things, a coconut, was about to be put into the hands of the president. Obama's security detail had a moment of panic. The coconut was whisked away by embarrassed and nervous agents to the contained X-ray facility where it was declared safe, re-wrapped, and handed back to the Hamiltons. Clutching their trouble-making gift, they were duly ushered into their

Oval Office meeting with their new black president. Mr Obama graciously accepted his coconut promising to find 'a real special place for it'. At which point Mrs Hamilton hugged Mr Obama and promised she would never clean the clothes that had come in contact with him – the same promise that Monica Lewinsky had famously made to herself in Bill Clinton's White House.

One magnificent piece of coconut sculpture has come from the hands of Zhang Xingfu. Zhang, now in his 70s, begins his day sitting near the window to take advantage of the morning light, something he has been doing for the past fifty years. Scraping and chipping with gentle precision, the wrinkled skin of his fingers echoing the undulations of his design on the nut, Zhang turns a coconut he bought in the market into an exquisitely carved hollow ball that intrigues and dazzles. Unlike the factory workers of Guangdong who turn out coconut buttons by the millions and almost as many plastic replicas of palms and nuts, Zhang is a master of coconut carving. He lives in Haikou, the port and capital of Hainan Island Province, China's southernmost outpost some 300 miles south-west of Hong Kong. His home is full of prized examples of his work. As a boy he enjoyed drawing and by the time he was 13 he was expanding his artistic talents into sculpting. He was paid just 15 yuan a month, he says, but he was happy. And he was a perfectionist: it was three years before he allowed anyone to see a finished carved coconut. 'I didn't care about the pay. I was just happy that I was learning something that was related to drawing.' It now takes about a month to produce a single carving. The factory Zhang first worked in received many orders before the 1980s – most for tourist souvenirs. But Zhang considered that there was more to his craft than tourist tat and continued to study with three established coconut carvers. He was not going to have his creative individuality smothered by the communist state. The dedication paid off when Zhang was chosen to work for a year on a commemorative vase made from coconut shells for the government of Hainan Province. It was presented by the provincial government to Macao as a gift in 1999 when the Portuguese formally handed control of their outpost back to China. The vase stands nearly 2m tall, weighs 80kg and comprises some 5000 coconut shells.

Coconut carving is a low-cost craft compared with sculpting with bronze. The shells are bought at market for about 5 yuan (70 cents) each, and Zhang is expert at discerning the best for shape, colour and hardness. While Zhang is clearly a craftsman and is concerned with individual decorative items, a local industry in household products fashioned from coconuts has blossomed in recent years. Tea sets made from coconut shell, coconut wine goblets, coconut vases, bowls, spoons, spatulas and lampshades have morphed from craft items into factory goods. However, the nuts may soon be harder to come by. Hainan does not produce enough coconuts to satisfy demand and a smuggling operation bringing seedlings from the Philippines has been making up the numbers. According to reports in the Philippine press in 2016, partially de-husked coconuts are shipped from the island of Leyte to Hainan via middlemen in Cebu, breaking customs regulations and undermining the Philippine economy in what some describe as an act of sabotage.

With a limit to the numbers of coconut palms that Hainan can produce, the Philippines are guaranteed what has become a fast-expanding export market. But selling the seedlings to the Chinese puts the market for the fully-grown nuts at risk, hence the smuggling operation. One estimate suggests that the brokers on Cebu are illegally handling 200,000 coconuts a day, paying farmers around 12 pesos per seedling and selling them on to the Chinese at 50 pesos each. With 3 million of the country's 12 million hectares of farmland devoted to growing coconuts and at least 25 per cent of the population dependent or partly dependent on coconuts for their livelihoods, selling seedlings to an export market is clearly not in the national interest, and the authorities in the Philippines are working to stamp it out.

Zhang's coconuts are still of the indigenous variety as are those of his craftsmen colleagues who turn coconuts into musical instruments. The *yehu* is a bowed two-string instrument with a sound box made from a coconut shell with the bow hair passing between the two strings. Similar instruments have been around since the Tang dynasty (618–907) They are popular in southern China as an accompanying instrument in classical Cantonese music in which only seven notes are used. The *banhu* is similar but found in the north of China where it is used to accompany folk opera. The neck is normally around 70cm long and made of rosewood. The two strings are tuned a fifth or a fourth apart, and the combination of the coarse horsehair bow and the resonating coconut chamber produces a sound characteristic of *glissando*, the permanent slide up or down between two notes.

Indian musicians use a similar instrument which they call a *ravanahatha*. The bowl or sound box is made of coconut shell covered with goat hide; the two strings, one of steel and the other of horsehair, are played with a long bow with little bells attached. The instrument originated in what is now Sri Lanka, was brought to India and reached the north of the country where it is used in Rajasthan as part of folk ensembles. The *ektara* is a simple one-string instrument popular with wandering minstrels and fakirs, itinerant ascetics. It too is made from a coconut shell with bamboo forming the neck. The *bin*, a similar instrument and popular with wandering minstrels in Assam, has the coconut shell resonator covered with the skin of a small mammal such as a frog or an iguana.

The *sarod* is altogether a more sophisticated instrument. Used in Hindustani classical music, it is similar to a lute with as many as twenty-five strings. Smaller than a sitar it sits comfortably in the player's lap and owes its modernity to six generations of the

An *ektara* with its coconut shell soundbox. (© The author)

Ali Khan family who have modified and perfected the instrument over several hundred years. Their wood of choice is teak. The steel strings (they were of silk originally) are plucked by a plectrum of polished coconut shell. The *sarod* has playing strings and drone strings. The four playing strings are plucked, and the drone strings vibrate at the same time producing a continuous echo-like effect. Amjad, the current head of the Ali Khan family, has played his *sarod* the world over – in London's Albert Hall, in the opera house in Sydney, at the Kennedy Centre, in the hallowed Palace of Westminster and at the Mozart Hall in Frankfurt. He composed *Tribute to Hong Kong*, with a major part for the *sarod*, for the Hong Kong Philharmonic Orchestra and its conductor Yoshikazu Fukumora. 'There is no essential difference between classical and popular music,' Mr Ali Khan contends. 'Music is music. I want to communicate with the listener who finds Indian classical music remote.' The *sarod* is commonly accompanied by the *tabla*, two drums played by the same performer. Both drums have compound skins onto which a tuning paste, or *siyahi*, is added to help generate the wide variety of tones these drums can produce. A concert of Hindustani classical music will last for an hour or more, beginning with improvisation from the soloist – often a *sarod* player. The composition follows – with improvised variations – but with a distinctive rhythm. The soloist is now joined by the *tabla* producing its own rhythms which will sometimes complement, but sometimes compete, in complex arrangements with the solo *sarod*. It is music not always easy on the ear for followers of Western classical music.

With an ear apparently well-tuned to Indian music is that most feared of all snakes, the cobra. The spitting, hissing Indian native has enough venom in its tiny sac to kill an elephant or at least twenty humans. Snake charmers in India and Pakistan, and increasingly elsewhere, entertain their passing audiences with dare-devil exploits as they charm their cobras from their baskets and risk their lives challenging them to lunge and hiss and bite.

But these snake charmers are charmers through and through. For a start they are not serenading their snakes. The seductive melodies from their flute-like instrument, the *pungi*, made with two bamboo tubes attached to a coconut shell containing reeds, might entertain the onlookers but do nothing for the snakes. The snakes are deaf. Taking the top off the basket is enough to make the snake curious and stick its head out. It might be encouraged by feet tapping on the ground. Once in the open, it follows the movement of the *pungi* while appearing to move with the music. Most charmers take no chances with these poisonous snakes. They either remove the sac containing the venom or they remove the fangs. And some remove both. But their audiences know none of this and continue to watch fearing and even willing the worst. Back in the early 1970s, the Indian government made keeping snakes illegal. But charmers are still called on to catch snakes when they appear on private land, and wildlife conservationists would rather have snakes captured than killed. But as the charmers lose their originality – and their credibility – their audiences are dwindling. Most charmers come from two lower castes for whom alternative ways of making a living are hard to find. The coconut and bamboo *pungi* is not played by anyone else, so like the snake charmers themselves, the instrument's days are numbered.

Not so the *sarod*. Much to everyone's surprise, the ancient instrument turned out to be the one featured in the score for the 2015 Bollywood hit movie *Piku*, a comedy drama about a man obsessed with his bowel movements who lives with his long-suffering daughter Piku. Given the wealth of coconuts in India and their role in so many rites and rituals, their regular appearance in films produced in the subcontinent is hardly surprising. While coconuts have been popular in Bollywood, they have been less in demand in Hollywood. For a first appearance, the coconut had to wait for the beginning of the talkies. *The Cocoanuts*, the Marx brothers' first full-length feature film adapted from the Irving Berlin Broadway musical, was set in the Hotel de Cocoanut on Palm Beach where the wrecked

Providencia had deposited its cargo of coconuts 51 years earlier. The cargo of coconuts swept up onto the Florida beach from the abandoned freighter gave that part of Florida, and the hotel itself, their names. The film contains the Irving Berlin classic 'Always' and a wonderful Groucho Marx line which went something like: 'You want ice water in room 202? I'll send up an onion. That'll make your eyes water.' A background role came for coconuts when MGM came looking for a follow-up for Howard Keel's screen debut in *Annie Get Your Gun*. They found it in *Pagan Love Song*, casting Keel as a quiet schoolteacher from Ohio who arrives in Tahiti to take over his late uncle's coconut plantation. But the coconuts pay second fiddle to the blossoming love affair between Keel's schoolteacher and a Tahitian beauty played by Esther Williams.

The coconut came of age sexually with the love affair between two teenagers in *Ventos de Agosto* (*August Winds*) the Brazilian documentary film-maker Gabriel Mascaro's first departure into film drama. Set in a small coconut-producing coastal village in Brazil, the film contemplates life and death through the lives of Jeison (Geova Manoel Dos Sanchos) and his girlfriend Shirley played by Dandera de Morais, the only professional actor in the cast. By day Shirley drives her father's truck hauling coconuts and after work cares for her ailing grandmother. With strict and conservative parents, Shirley and Jeison are forced to spend intimate moments together high up and out of sight on the coconuts piled high on her father's trailer. Mascaro co-wrote the film with Rachel Ellis, a graduate of the London School of Economics who worked in international development before turning to cinema and moving to Brazil. Mascaro and Ellis found the ideal setting for their film in a coastal village surrounded by coconut plantations on Brazil's north coast within reach of Reciffe, Mascaro's home town. They told the villagers they needed people to act in their film, and on the day set for the auditions, the whole village turned up – with the exception of a certain Geova Dos Santos who presented himself ruefully two days later asking if there might be a role for him. Mascaro told him to sing something on camera, and promptly signed him up on the spot for the male lead. *August Winds,* with a running time of just seventy-seven minutes, and produced on a very modest budget, was released at the Locarno Film Festival in 2014 to quietly complimentary reviews. It was screened at the London Film Festival that same year but failed to gain distribution for general release. (See p.4 of colour section.)

While providing great background to *August Winds*, the nut finally landed a starring role with a sketch in *Monty Python and the Holy Grail*, creating one of the most memorable scenes in film history. The 1975 comedy, based on the legend of King Arthur and his search for the Holy Grail, was made by the British comedy team of Graham Chapman, John Cleese, Terry Gilliam, Eric Idle, Terry Jones, and Michael Palin, with Gilliam and Jones directing. In the opening scene, Arthur the pillar of chivalry, King of the Britons (Graham Chapman) appears riding an imaginary horse like a child with a broom between its legs in the school playground. With him is his servant Patsy (Terry Gilliam) who knocks two coconut halves together to make the sound of their imaginary horses' hooves. They arrive out of the mist at a castle where the following conversation takes place with a guard on the castle wall – a much-loved piece of dialogue Python fans will recite word-for-word without a single prompt. 'Who goes there?' shouts the guard, at which a conversation ensues between the king and the guard, with the guard accusing the king of being an imposter and pointing out that, far from riding horses, the king and his servant are using coconut halves to simulate the sound of horses' hooves. The king, not surprisingly affronted by the guard's lack of respect, persists. But the guard will have none of it: 'Where'd you get the coconuts?' he asks. The king replies they found them, whereupon the guard, sensing he is gaining the intellectual upper hand, points out that coconuts are a tropical fruit while the part of the world they inhabit happens to be in a temperate zone. Holding his ground, the king educates the guard in the habits of migrating birds suggesting these high flyers could have carried the nuts. But the guard does not buy the idea of a 5oz swallow carrying a 1lb coconut and takes his turn to educate the king in the aerodynamics involved in the beating of a swallow's wings and air-speed velocity.

The film cost US $400,000 and took US $5 million at the box office. In America ABC television viewers named it the best comedy of all time in their *Greatest Movies of Our Time* show in 2011. British audiences were not quite so enthusiastic, with Channel 4 television viewers putting the film at number six in their best comedy list. In 2005 the film had already spawned a Tony Award-winning Broadway musical spinoff, *Spamalot.* Written primarily by Eric Idle, and directed by Mike Nichols, it opened on Broadway at the Shubert Theatre in March of 2005 to rave reviews and won the Tony Award for Best Musical. Its West End premiere at the Palace Theatre on London's Cambridge Circus came in October 2006 with the Shakespearian actor Simon Russell Beale taking over the lead from Tim Curry early the following year. The audience roared its approval.

To mark the first anniversary of the Broadway opening, the world's largest coconut orchestra, 1,789 people clapping together half coconut shells, performed in Shubert Alley, outside the theatre. The 'orchestra' was officially recognised by the *Guinness Book of World Records*. London was not to be outdone. On St George's Day in 2007, 5,500 Monty Python fans filed into Trafalgar Square. They all had with them their two halves of a coconut. From the plinth that supports Admiral Nelson, the London cast of *Spamalot,* with Terry Gilliam and Terry Jones and with London's then mayor Ken Livingstone in support, led the fans in a rousing coconutty version of the show's hit song 'Always Look on the Bright Side of Life'. Lord Nelson might have pirouetted on his column if he had not already turned in his grave. On the ground, impressed by the size of the gathering rather than its musical talent, the head of Guinness World Records declared a new record for a coconut orchestra.

Six years later, things turned a little sour. In 2013 the Pythons lost a legal case against Mark Forstater, the film's producer, over royalties for Eric Idle's derivative work, *Spamalot*. They owed a combined £800,000 in legal fees and back royalties to Forstater. To help cover the cost of these royalties and fees, the group arranged and performed in a stage show, *Monty Python Live (Mostly)* held at the O2 arena in London in July 2014. Python fans who cycle and can't let go of their comedy heroes and their horse-less King Arthur, can now fit a wooden mechanical device that sits on top of the front wheel, making a sound like a horse. The device is constructed from empty halves of a coconut shell that clop together.

2018 saw the premiere of a play by the British-Pakistani writer Guleraana Mir. She called her play *Coconut*. The word coconut had become something of an insult amongst immigrant communities describing someone who betrayed their heritage by pandering to white opinion – brown on the outside and white on the inside like a coconut. (A court in 2010 saw a black city councillor in Bristol in the west of England accused of racial harassment after calling an Asian political opponent a 'coconut'. Magistrates found the councillor Shirley Brown guilty as charged and gave her a twelve-month conditional discharge and ordered her to pay costs.) Guleraana had herself suffered the insult and had written her play for 'all the brown girls who are struggling to come to terms with where they belong'. She describes herself as a non-practising Muslim, and asks what a 'coconut' can do when it comes to finding love. In her teens she feared God might be watching if she acted on her desire for boys, and as an adult, discovered that white men found her exotic but recoiled at her ethnic practices. And as for brown men, they were far too controlling. Basing her play on her own experiences, she produced a dark comedy which both informs and entertains as it explores the experiences of Asian women in contemporary Britain. *Coconut*, a novel by the South African writer Kopano Matlwa, covers similar ground to Gulraana as it chronicles the lives of two black women growing up in a white suburb, and struggling to find their identities.

Few poets have chosen the palm or its fruit as the focus for their work, but from Africa comes a gentle and informative, but unattributed, Swahili poem discovered at the beginning of the twentieth century amongst a collection of old marriage songs:

> Give me the minstrel's seat that I may sit at ease and tell of the praises of the coco-palm. This tree, when it is young and sprouting, spreads its leaves outwards widely.
>
> Then it thrusts forth its bole and puts forth its leaf sheath and its spreading roots, lastly it brings forth its fruits, and its fruits are known as coconuts.
>
> They are plucked down and stripped of their husks and cooked with boiled rice and sauces, from the empty shell, they carve a ladle for cooking for the servant girl Sada.
>
> Its grated nut, squeezed free of juice, is scattered on the midden and the cock scratches for it there, its fibre they plait into cord for the rigging of clippers and dhows
>
> With its fronds they thatch a house and ward off the winds and the wind-swept sand, of its trunk they make doors to resist the enemy and the robber at one's gate.

8

FOR GOD AND COUNTRY

Kerala is one of the smaller states of the world's largest democracy. It occupies a narrow stretch of India's south-western coastal region from the border with Karnataka in the north to its border with Tamil Nadu at the country's southern tip. From the Malabar coast where its shores are washed by the Arabian Sea it stretches inwards and upwards to the undulating tea plantations of the Western Ghats. It has a population of some 35 million that boasts the highest literacy rate in all of India. Keralans are a mixture of Hindus, Muslims and Christians who live together in remarkable harmony. They speak their own language – Malayalam. In Malayalam, Kerala means 'coconut place' or 'land of coconuts'. And for good reason. Kerala has more land devoted to coconut palms than anywhere else in India, producing billions of coconuts – more than 5 billion annually – and defining the livelihoods of large parts of the population and at the same time prompting change in the patriarchal social mores of the nation.

While one of the two genetically distinct groups of coconut clearly had its beginnings in Southeast Asia, the other can be traced to the shores of southwest India. The oldest coconut fossils have been found here. The palms found ideal conditions in the tropical temperatures and rainfall, and flourished from day one. Tens of millions of palms define the lowlands and backwaters of the state. Passengers travelling through Kerala on the *Bangalore Express* find their glassless windows framing coconut palms for mile after mile after mile as the train trundles north, ceaselessly hooting a warning to people for whom the railway track is home and coconuts are food and drink. (See p.16 of colour section.)

Local people have long relied on the coconut palm not just for food but for shelter too. They roofed their homes with the palm's fronds, drank the nut's water and fed off the highly nutritious white meat. They made fires for cooking from the husk, and the empty nuts were halved and used as drinking cups. At home women spun the fibres of the husk into string and rope and matting. Even today this woven husk, or coir, is India's most important coconut product. The coir fills a host of consumer products from mattresses to car seats and mattings. Wipe your feet on your doormat and the chances are you will be wiping your feet on Indian coconut coir. Competitors at the 2008 Olympics in Beijing slept on Indian coir mattresses. European car makers upholster seats with pads of coir bonded with rubber latex. Hop growers in the United States use coir twine to tie up their vines, and with the natural fibre being resistant to salt water, it makes excellent nets for catching shellfish. In Australia they use coir pith as an absorbent to clean up oil spills. And its durability, hairy texture, ability to hold water and the fact that it is biodegradable make it an attractive geotextile for soil erosion control. Road builders have long used geosynthetics, but engineers now suggest that sustainable coir geotextiles can do the job equally well, helping to absorb the constant impact of vehicles and thus extending a road's life.

It was the Tata company – the Indian steel maker – that first saw the potential for industrialising coconut products on the subcontinent. A century ago, in 1917, Dorab Tata, the British educated son of the firm's Parsee founder Jamsetji Tata, established India's first coconut oil mill at Cochin on the Kerala backwaters. The local economy was in poor shape, and the mill created new jobs, and a ready market for families with coconut palms. The business also pioneered the employment of women, providing jobs in administration and in the mill's laboratories – a move that proved unwelcome amongst the male employees. And it was at the mill that India's first cooperative movement took shape. Coconuts were driving gender politics and labour relations, and when the company started using its coconut oil to make soap, the nut was driving the business agenda too.

Householders now had a new soap that was still cheap but that lathered easily. (Indians had been used to using gram flour (ground chickpeas) as a cleansing agent until the first soaps were made at Meerut in central north India by the North West Soap Company at the end of the nineteenth century.) Lever Brothers began selling soap in India, and by 1934 were making it in the country too. When Tata entered the soap business both companies were selling their boxes of soap cakes for ten rupees until Lever triggered a price war. By the time the price had dropped to 6 rupees a box, Tata was on its knees. There was much gnashing of teeth, but the Indians hung on, and within three months Lever Brothers had brought their price back in line with Tata's 10 rupees. Gandhi's 'swadeshi' movement – the encouragement of domestic goods and boycott of imported ones – gave the Tata soap the moral high ground and the local company set about improving its marketing and eventually building six more mills.

Its rivalry with Lever Brothers, however, was not over. M.O. Matthai was at the time Jawaharlal Nehru's secretary. In his book *My Days with Nehru* he recounts how a ban on imported cosmetics caused outrage amongst India's middle-class women who besieged the prime minister's house, asking why their much-needed cosmetics could not be manufactured in India. Nehru's daughter Indira Gandhi who was acting as her father's hostess and personal assistant, was sympathetic and at one point chided Matthai for failing to understand the gravity of the matter. Letters and telegrams from women all over India were stacked on the prime minister's desk. Exasperated, Matthai summoned Tata's local director in Delhi – K.A.D. Naoroji. Matthai was nothing if not direct with the businessman. India's women were up in arms, he explained, unable to get their hands on all the beauty products they needed, so wasn't it time Tata went into the cosmetics business? While there was no beating about the bush from Nehru's right-hand man, there was hesitation in Naoroji's eyes. Matthai, clearly mindful of his boss' desk swamped with the letters of the country's vain women, was the first to blink. If Tata gave Indian women what they wanted, the company could expect every bit of assistance from the government. The deal was done and approved by the then group chairman Jehangir Tata. They called the new cosmetics company Lakme and with French collaboration (Jehangir's mother was French) a range of sophisticated beauty products were being snapped up by women across the subcontinent. In time, however, the Tata board decided that cosmetics were really not part of their core products – the steel, cars, engineering, power, white goods – and sold the company to its old rival Lever Brothers now constituted as Hindustan Lever, in whose hands the company continues to thrive.

While the coconuts of southern India find their way into some of today's markets, it is the coir that earns the majority of the foreign exchange. But the industry is in need of modernisation. Extracting fibre from the coconut husk has traditionally been a cottage industry and largely in the hands of women. And while it provides employment, the system is far from efficient. In an effort to protect jobs, India's powerful trades unions have made the introduction of mechanised processing difficult for local companies, and while coir processing plants do exist, even they rely on homeworkers to remove the husk from the shell. India's agriculture sector remains backward. There is a twenty-four-hour state-run TV channel for farmers but farming practices have changed little over the years. As the country's population expands (India is fast closing in on China as the world's most populous nation) the size of land plots decrease, and this is exacerbated by state laws that limit the area of farmland an individual can own. This holds productivity back, on top of which mechanisation in coconut farming hardly exists. With one recent exception.

Meet Soma Rajan. Soma is 53, married with two children. He left school at 14 and began his working life on the dockside in Cochin, loading and unloading the cargo ships. But for the last twenty years he has been picking coconuts. His dark, weathered skin pays testament to the hours he spends under the sun. His high cheek bones protrude over sunken cheeks, his hair is thick, black and shiny (he treats it with coconut oil every morning) and long wiry hairs grow from his ears. He smiles easily despite the morning's efforts which have left sweat sticking his grey shirt to his chest. Soma is part of Kerala's gig economy, moving from one plantation to another when he is needed. Until five years ago, Soma would climb a coconut palm with bare feet and just a piece of coir rope in a loop around his ankles. Now he has the one piece of mechanisation to come to the aid of pickers. It is a pair of glorified climbing crampons designed by students at a local agricultural university. A ratchet system at each step makes climbing easier, and a belt around the tree makes it safer. Even so, picking is not without its dangers, especially when the wind gets up and the 80ft trees begin to bend and sway.

Soma cycles to work and is ready to start climbing shortly after dawn, and works through until 4.00 p.m. in the afternoon. On average he will climb thirty trees in an hour cutting down around

Soma Rajan, defined by his white head scarf. (© The author)

300 nuts. He charges 40 rupees per tree (the equivalent of 40p or 55 US cents). With three colleagues he looks after some 100,000 trees on the island of Kallenchen in the Kerala backwaters. He and his fellow pickers belong to the Velan caste – a caste of some 86,000 Hindus which has traditionally been associated with coconut picking and clothes washing. Together he and his friends make the annual pilgrimage to Sabarimala having first fasted for forty-one days denying themselves meat, alcohol, cigarettes and sex. The supplicant must bathe every morning but must not shave, and he must devote his time to prayer and good works. A little sheepishly, Soma also admits to smashing coconuts when he goes to his temple. It is not just when he needs Ganesh to help him through

some problem or other: he breaks coconuts at the temple simply to please Ganesh. If the coconut fails to break when it hits the stone floor? … Soma smiles again. 'It has to,' he says.

Soma's father was a coconut picker but he doubts that his children will follow him into picking. The younger generation's preference for life in the cities and for skilled jobs that command better wages is a problem for the coconut industry. Without machines to do the picking, the industry still relies on manpower – and now too on womanpower. Government agencies in southern India have been recruiting pickers and for the first time have been targeting women. India has a poor record for bringing women into the workplace. According to the *Economist* newspaper just 26 per cent of women in India go out to work. Patriarchal social mores discourage women from working unless the family finances give them little choice. When this happens it only reinforces the stigma attached to working women: a family whose women stay at home are seen as being on a respectable rung of the social ladder.

None of this prevented Manju Suresh from enrolling on a state-funded course for coconut pickers – even if her reasons for doing so were not in answer to the labour shortage. (She was pregnant with her first child and she developed a craving for coconut water.) But those patriarchal social mores almost prevented her from signing on. It was her elder brother who took exception, telling his sister that coconut picking was not a job for a woman. Manju feared her husband might have the same attitude and she began to wonder whether to give it all up. But her husband came round to the idea, and Manju duly signed on. When she reached the top of her first tree she admits it was frightening being so high. But with a giggle, she says the view from the top was so great she did not want to come down.

Manju is an experienced picker now, able to fell 120 nuts from a single tree in less than ten minutes. She hooks her *vakkathi* (a small machete) in her waistband at the back letting the blade rest just above her buttocks, and in minutes is up amongst the

Manju Suresh: woman in a man's world. (© The author)

coconuts cutting away at their stems. As she works, a telephone rings from somewhere inside her folds of clothes. It is a new client. She makes a mental note of the location, tucks the phone away and gets on with the job in hand. Word of mouth brings all the cutting she needs. She is paid 50 rupees per tree and covers forty trees in her working day. She taught her husband how to use the new climbing devices and the pair now work together using their Enfield motorbike to travel between the plantations and home – a one-room apartment they share with their two children. She is clearly proud of what she has achieved. God, she says, made it possible, and she gives coconuts to her church as an offering. While plantation work brings in the money, no job is too small for pickers like Soma and Manju. Tens of thousands of homeowners in southern India boast two or three palms on their land. They rely on the self-employed pickers and extract enough oil from the flesh of the nuts for their own domestic use and sell any surplus at local markets.

Neither Soma nor Manju are members of a union. Sajeevan, on the other hand, had no choice. He belongs to a union affiliated to the Communist Party of India. There are benefits, to be sure, and a pension, but strikes were a regular feature of membership and at times it seemed as if they were pricing themselves out of business. Sajeevan is not a picker: he is a tapper. He taps the flower of the palm before it produces its nuts to extract the sap which ferments into alcohol they call toddy. Sajeevan climbs his trees the old way with just a loop of rope around his ankles to provide the tension to hold his feet against the trunk. He takes a buffalo bone from his waistband and with it tenderises the flower. Then he makes small incisions in the flesh of the flower and places a clay pot around it to collect the sap. The longer the sap is left to ferment the more potent it becomes.

Toddy tappers work with permits from the local licensing authority. Yet, in what appears to be in direct opposition to licensing, the state is trying to reduce alcohol consumption. Keralans drink more than anyone else in India, and alcoholism and alcohol-related illness have become a major problem for legislators. The age limit for alcohol consumption has been raised to 23, but the rise has had little effect on teenage drinking which is reaching crisis levels. Toddy is commonly 8 per cent alcohol, and a 750ml bottle sells in a toddy shop for just 50 rupees (50p or 70 US cents). Sajeevan is one of some 30,000 toddy tappers in Kerala, and restrictions on the sale of toddy would impact on this significant proportion of the workforce. Toddy shops are popular amongst blue collar workers and considered part of Keralan culture. Any attempt to close them down would face determined opposition – not only from the tappers and their union representatives.

Raja carrying a bunch of nuts. (© The author)

India has been slow to respond to worldwide demand for coconut products. The shortage of pickers, the unions' opposition to mechanisation which, they say, poses a threat to jobs, and a government in Delhi failing to address the needs of farmers, have all mitigated against plantation owners developing their businesses. Shaji Palathingal is an exception. In 2007 he bought 100 acres of land on Kerala's border with Tamil Nadu at the foot of the Western Ghats. With the help of a team of coolies, he and his uncle planted 5000 carefully chosen seedlings. Those seedlings have grown into 80ft trees each of which is currently producing 150 nuts every year. His pickers like Raja do not climb: they keep their feet firmly on the ground using bamboo poles topped with crescent-shaped knives to fell the nuts. Raja earns one rupee for every nut, and typically comes with his wife who collects the nuts and carries them in a basket on her head to collecting points where she loads the nuts onto tractor trailers.

Shaji's confidence in the coconut industry comes with the knowledge that the domestic market provides financial security, worldwide demand for coconut oil remains strong, and coconut charcoal is finding ever more uses. Furthermore, palms produce several batches of nuts in a twelve-month period unlike most other crops that mature just once a year and are prone to adverse weather conditions. (A crop failure deprives a farmer of his livelihood and plunges him into debt and despair. Suicide, all too prevalent in India and the leading cause of death amongst Indians between the ages of 15 and 39, is particularly common amongst farming communities.)

Shaji's use of bamboo pluckers to fell the nuts is more efficient than using climbers. A plucker, his wife and a third family member will collect 10,000 nuts in a single day. And coconuts can be stored without any loss of quality. (In the regions of southern India where the unions are particularly powerful, the use of bamboo poles is banned because it deprives the less efficient climbers of jobs.) There is always the risk of the traders hoarding nuts to create an artificial shortage and push up the price. Shaji sells to traders he trusts but they drive a hard bargain and give him and growers like him little alternative in getting their coconuts to the processing companies. Each of his palms give him 150 nuts each year – a yield he intends to increase with good husbandry to 200. An irrigation system guards against periods of low rainfall. Pests, however, can be a problem. The red palm weevil can destroy a coconut palm in a month. The adult female lays up to 300 eggs in holes it makes in the tree's trunk. The larvae then eat their way up and down the inside of the tree destroying it unseen.

While Shaji has put his faith in a plantation, smallholders are facing a dilemma. Sajeer, who works in a hotel restaurant, lived with his mother in a house shaded by four coconut palms. They had nuts in abundance, extracting the oil and making milk from the white flesh. Surplus nuts were sold at 30 rupees each (30p or 40 US cents). But such is the demand for land in Kerala, and particularly in Cochin and its environs, that plots with the space to support palms are being sold to developers who cut down the trees and squeeze in extra accommodation. P.K. Thampan was, until his retirement, the chairman of India's Coconut Development Board. He is 86 now and still boasts a head covered in healthy black hair – the result of plastering it with coconut oil every day of his life. He wears a *dhoti*, a greying T-shirt, and sandals. Ten palms served his household well, he says. Home-grown palms were the source of livelihood even for families living on the smallest plots. But now he sees the need for better husbandry and he laments the shortage of pickers. Monkeys, considered highly efficient coconut pickers in Thailand, are not used in India, and picking, says Thampan, is now considered a low station job. 'Things have to change,' said a young attentive visitor, and P.K. Thampan agreed by shaking his head.

While India clearly needs to make changes to realise the commercial potential of its huge coconut crop, tradition has secured the nut's place at the heart of the nation's spiritual needs. One billion men, women and children adhere to Hindu beliefs, and 90 per cent of them live in India. Ethics, myth and ritual rule their daily lives, and these numerous and vital rituals are almost always centred on coconuts. Just how coconuts came to have such a central role in Hindu customs still puzzles historians. One clue lies in the time-honoured practice of sacrifice which plays an important role in Hinduism. The rituals associated with sacrifice have evolved over several thousand years even though the Vedic texts are supposed to dictate and lay down the rules. There is a history of blood sacrifice, particularly in the worship of the goddess Kali, the slayer of evil who has an appetite for blood. It was only 200 years ago that in Calcutta's Kali temple, a male child was sacrificed daily. Hindu mythology has it that the sage Vishvamitra created the coconut in part to appease the deities and put a stop to human and animal sacrifice, and some believers point to the three germination pores at the base of the nut which gives the fruit the appearance of a human face. Devotees still flock to the Kali temples today, but coconuts instead of male children are used in the sacrificial rite. And throughout Hinduism the coconut has become a symbol of sacrifice. Hindus keep the physical practice, and 'slaughter' a whole coconut by cracking the nut open, believing the fruit and flowers are substitutes for animals.

Hinduism is more a set of beliefs than a faith while for some it is simply a way of life. No particular founder has been identified and there are no written scriptures that could be compared to the Bible, the Koran or the Torah, although for many Hindus the Vedic texts provide the philosophical background to their beliefs. There are no priests in the Christian sense, and while there is one true god, Hindus worship Him through a huge choice of deities.

However, while daily human sacrifices are no more, newspaper reports suggest that in some parts of the Hindu world, animal and human sacrifice does still exist – if not on a daily basis. *The Guardian* newspaper reported in 2006 the sacrificing of a 3-year-old boy in India's poverty-stricken province of Khurja in Uttar Pradesh. Sumitra Bushan, who was 43, led a wretched existence and was plagued by nightmares of the goddess Kali. She consulted a travelling 'holy man' who suggested she sacrifice a chicken. When this did not work and the screaming nightmares continued, the 'holy man' bade her make a further sacrifice: 'sacrifice another – a boy from your village'. So with the help of her two sons, she kidnapped her neighbour's son, performed a *puja* (a prayer ritual) and then after smearing sandalwood paste and globules of ghee over the terrified child's body, encouraged her sons to cut off the child's ears, nose and hands, before leaving him before the image of the goddess Kali, bleeding to death.

Animal sacrifices are more common but still avoided by the majority of Hindu sects – with one startling exception. The Sanskrit word for animal sacrifice is *bali*, meaning tribute or offering, and it is in this spirit that ritual sacrifices, particularly of goats, are performed. At one festival in Nepal, which occurs every five years in honour of Gadhimai the goddess of power, the act of sacrifice takes on a whole new meaning. In the space of two days more than 100,000 cattle, buffaloes, chicken, goats and even rats are decapitated within the temple walls at the village of Bariyarpur, turning the scorched earth into a grotesque killing field of thousands of headless animals, with streams of blood curling through the sand and dust. If animal rights activists get their way, the next event, scheduled for 2019, will be a very different affair.

The majority of Hindus have long disapproved of both these practices, partly because many don't eat meat and because of their belief in non-violence. In the vast majority of Hindu sects, it is the coconut that is generally regarded as a metaphor for humans and animals. The nut is the most common offering at Hindu temples, and dozens of rituals have coconuts at the heart of the ceremony. Smashing a coconut signifies the smashing of the ego and exposing the purity of the inner self (coconut water is as pure a fluid as you will find) in preparation for facing god. It is considered auspicious to break coconuts at the start of a new business, at weddings, at the beginning of a long journey, and when laying the foundations of a new house.

Once a month at a temple in the Kanur district of Tamil Nadu in the south east of India, Hindu devotees young and old, male and female, sit in line to have a coconut broken on their heads in honour of the goddess Lakshmi. Neurosurgeons have warned of the risks, but the chance to please the goddess of wealth, fortune and prosperity is too good to miss, and medical tents are available for when things go wrong. This monthly ritual, so locals tell, stems from colonial times when the British wanted to route a new railway through the grounds of the village temple. The village objected and the engineers jokingly suggested that if any of the villagers could break the large stones on which the track was to be laid, they would change the route. When local men did just that, the railway company had no option but to honour its word. The line now runs 1.5km north of the 800-year-old temple.

Across the state border in Kerala, more coconuts are smashed, this time in honour of Lords Ayyappan and Vettakkorumakan.

But this time the nuts, thousands of them, are smashed on the ground by a single individual spurred on by two trained drummers beating devotional rhythmic encouragement. The oracle, as he is called, uses alternate hands, raising his arms high above his head before swinging them down releasing the coconut onto the stone in front of him. His helpers keep the coconuts coming. Relentlessly, one coconut after another, sweat glistening on his naked torso, his mind in a state of absolute devotion, he smashes the nuts onto the ground. Manoj Kumar Kandamangalam was 16 when he took on the work of an oracle. His skill and stamina keep him in constant demand at temples across southern India. His family is one among a handful of Brahmin families with the right to practice the ritual which Manoj sees as being something of an art as well as a religious practice. At each ceremony he is expected to smash 12,000 coconuts. When he first began to perform the ritual it took him more than four hours to work through all 12,000 nuts. When he got it down to two hours and thirteen minutes they put him in the *Limca Book of Records*, India's version of the *Guinness Book of Records*. Now in his 30s, Manoj told an Indian newspaper that once he got immersed in the art of it, the process became effortless and enjoyable. And if his sons wanted to follow in their father's footsteps, he would not be standing in their way.

The deity Ayyappam is fêted with coconuts by those followers who make the annual pilgrimage to Sabarimala, high in the forests of Kerala's Western Ghats. To stand face to face with their deity, the devout must climb 1,500ft barefoot and stripped to the waist up a steep, rocky path through a tiger reserve in temperatures reaching 30°C. On their climb they pass huts selling water, and tents equipped as field hospitals with volunteer doctors, beds, oxygen and heart monitors. (I have climbed with them and the field hospitals are a welcome sight.) On their heads they carry their *irumudi*, a bag of hand-woven cotton cloth containing a coconut filled with ghee (clarified butter). In the bag's second compartment are two further coconuts along with ginger, turmeric, and betel leaves. Once at the temple and having climbed the final eighteen gold-covered sacred steps, the pilgrim's final act is to experience *darshan*, to have sight of their deity. The ghee from the first coconut is ritualistically poured over the deity, and the coconut smashed and tossed into the *Aazhi*, a huge fire bowl.

Sabarimala, and its coconuts, has become the focus for bitter arguments about the relationship in India between women, religion and the state. Tradition has prevented women between the ages of 10 and 50 from worshipping at the temple because of ideas about impurity associated with menstruation. Time-honoured tradition was set in law in 1991 when the High Court of Kerala banned women of menstruating age from entering the temple grounds. But this ban was challenged in 2006 by the Indian Young Lawyers Association who argued that the ban violated article 25 of the Constitution that gave the freedom to everyone to follow their religion. After being dragged through the courts for twelve years the Indian Supreme Court finally overturned the ban in 2018 pitting the courts and the state against a patriarchal society that places huge emphasis on tradition and religious beliefs. There were state-wide protests against the Supreme Court ruling culminating in a general strike. Of the five judges who delivered the ruling one, a woman, dissented. The courts, she said, had no place in the realms of religious beliefs.

Hundreds of thousands of coconut-carrying devotees make their way to Sabarimala every year with dozens needing medical attention during the final climb. But the numbers of coconuts offered to their chosen deity during this demanding pilgrimage pales into insignificance when compared with the quantities sent as offerings to the Maa Tarini temple at Ghatgaon in the eastern Indian province of Orissa. Some 15,000 coconuts arrive here every day filling the temple's storage facility designed to hold 350,000 nuts. The nuts are distributed amongst local tradesmen who make *Nadiakora*, a variety of coconut sweets, while any excess is left to rot outside. To many, this vast collection of coconuts appears a wasteful extravagance. But such is the faith in the powers of Maa Tarini, that offerings to the goddess remain a must for a growing number of devotees. The belief in her powers also facilitates what has become a unique free delivery service. Bus and lorry drivers in Orissa heading in the vague direction of Ghatgoan will pick up a coconut offering ringed with red ribbon from bystanders in the belief that by so doing their journeys will be blessed. Collection boxes at intersections across the state are used as transfer points connecting with services heading directly for the temple. And the service is guaranteed because no bus or lorry driver will refuse to carry the nuts for fear of offending Maa Tarini.

The breaking of coconuts at a personal level accompanies any new venture. A new home is blessed with the breaking of coconuts: a new car, new motorbikes, a new business are all attended by the breaking of a coconut. A bride will likely carry a lavishly decorated coconut to her wedding, and then there will be a coconut to celebrate her first pregnancy. Godh bharna is a significant event in the lives of Hindu married women. The ceremony which celebrates a woman's first pregnancy is held in the seventh month of the pregnancy. In Hindu mythology *godh* means the lap of the woman and *bharna* means to fill. So it is that the woman's mother and mother-in-law, dressed in all their celebratory finery place in her *godh* – her lap – a coconut marked with a red swastika. The swastika is an ancient religious symbol and, before it was hijacked by Hitler's Nazis, was widely revered by Hindus as a symbol representing the sun and energy. The Sanskrit term *svasti* translates roughly as 'well-being'. It is found on doors and walls of temples as well as being etched on coconuts at special occasions. It is also central to the followers of Jainism and appears on the Jain emblem. And it is an important symbol in Jain rituals just as it is for Hindus and Buddhists. (While it remains an important symbol in Asia, devotees living in the West have become hesitant to embrace the swastika because of the stigma attached to its connections with the Third Reich.) (See p.2 of colour section.)

Hindus believe in reincarnation. Death and cremation in the Hindu community are attended by rites and customs so numerous and complex that, when circumstances allow, preparations are set in motion well before death is certified. Families do all they can to make sure their relatives die not in hospital but at home where the necessary rituals that will ensure the onward journey of the spirit can be managed comfortably in accordance with Vedic traditions. Varanasi, on the banks of the Ganges, is where the most devout Hindus bring their dead, burning their corpses on funerial pyres before spreading the ashes on the river's sacred waters. Cremation here, Hindus believe, ensures immediate entry into heaven, preventing rebirth as anything other than a human being. The cremations are handled by members of the Dom, the untouchable caste responsible for such matters, who spend their lives surrounded by death from one generation to the next.

Life on the stone steps of the ghats where the pyres burn is joyless, unhealthy but lucrative. Corpses, wrapped in brightly-coloured shrouds covered with garlands of marigolds and carried on bamboo stretchers, arrive in a constant stream day and night. Relatives must pay for the wood they will burn – it will take up to 40 kilos to burn an average-sized body – and for the privilege of using the eternal holy flame from which they light their pyres. For this, the Dom will charge exorbitant amounts of money in the knowledge that his supplicants believe his flame will light the torch that has the power to guarantee the swift passage to heaven for their loved one. Bargaining is often protracted and heated. Finally, with negotiations complete, the corpse is immersed in the river's blackened polluted waters for a few moments. It is then left to dry before being covered with ghee and set on the pyre, the smell of burning flesh combining with the stench of animal dung and the city's raw sewage. Relatives place propitious coconuts on the burning pyre. But if they don't keep an eye on the pyre, children, seemingly immune to the heat of the flames and hidden in the swirling smoke, will sneak up to the fire, remove the coconuts with sticks, break the nuts open and feed off the white flesh. Local men who have been swimming in the river, stand by nonchalantly around the pyres drying off. When the body has become ash and the fire subsided, the youngsters are back to collect the charcoal for cooking, while *ganja* smokers stuff burning embers into their *chillums* or pipes. The next day, the Dom's servants will be back to sift through the ashes looking for gold or silver jewellery.

The funerial pyres at Varanasi consume huge quantities of wood. Given that Hindus everywhere else in India cremate their dead, even if not in such holy environments, the number of trees felled to supply the huge quantities of firewood runs into millions. And that has become a concern for India's environmentalists. In 2016 an initiative aimed at reducing the reliance on wood to cremate the country's dead was launched in the south of the country. According to the *Times of India* a group of volunteers in the city of Coimbatore, the centre of India's coconut industry, have come up with a scheme using coconut shells. The shell burns well and in a powdered form can be easily and cheaply transported. Discarded shells were collected from hotels, schools, residential complexes and marriage halls, and a first batch of 140 tonnes of pulverised shells was delivered to Varanasi, enough, say the organisers, to burn 2,800 bodies while saving as many as 2,000 trees. However, the scheme has already met with opposition from Varanasi's Doms who traditionally sell wood for the pyres, and from mourners who have doubts about coconuts burning their family members with the speed necessary to ensure a speedy passage to heaven. The environmentalists from Coimbatore say that it is early days. Gas-fired and electric crematoriums have already been tried at Varanasi and proved unpopular but, say the coconut enthusiasts, theirs is a natural product and, after all, simply a product of a tree.

Coconuts are in evidence again in the Hindu community in circumstances when there is no body to burn, when preparation for a cremation becomes even more elaborate. The deceased may have drowned, have died in some distant land, or may have died in circumstances that rendered the body too damaged or simply unsuitable for the sacrificial cremation. Nevertheless, the spirit needs to be cared for so a surrogate corpse must be assembled. And this process requires even more detailed and careful ritualistic preparation than a body. When we are born, our infant bodies contain about 300 bones. But as we grow older some of the smaller bones fuse and as adults our bone count goes down to 206. However, Vedic tradition requires the surrogate corpse to represent the deceased's life from birth, so the starting point for the effigy is a collection of 300 sticks or twigs from a palasa tree, a tree native to India with soft, off-white wood and popular with herbalists treating back pain. The twigs bound together constitute the body. A mature coconut serves as the head. Pig hair ensures the corpse is not bald, cowrie shells serve as eyes, a cotton fruit becomes the nose, a palm leaf acts as a tongue and pomegranate seeds suggest teeth. To finish it off, eyebrows are added using barley grass. This surrogate body is given a fleshy appearance by coating the twigs with barley paste followed by a mixture of cornflour and ghee, purified butter. This 'body', while lacking the capacity to perform physical activities, is now believed by its creators to be endowed with spiritual qualities. It receives the first of the life cycle rites – a ritual performed when a baby is conceived – then fifteen remaining rites are performed to transform the body of twigs into one that effectively represents the deceased, and which is ready for the rituals that normally take place between death and cremation. Only then is the 'deceased' ready for the funeral pyre.

Given the coconut's revered place in Hindu society, it is something of a shock to see it as the centrepiece of an unholy rough and tumble on India's north-eastern border with Burma. The fact that coconuts do not grow here only adds to the surprise. The state of Manipur (population 2.75 million) in the Himalayan hills, described by India's first Prime Minister Jawaharlal Nehru as the 'Jewel of India', has long been home to a seven-a-side game called *yubi lakpi* which translates in simple terms as coconut snatching. And in simple terms that is what the game is about. A large, oval-shaped coconut serves as a ball which match officials cover in grease to make things more challenging. On a pitch 45m long and 18m wide, the slippery nut must be carried over a central goal line and placed in the hands of an umpire dressed from head to foot in white. The players wear shorts with coloured waistbands but no shirts and no shoes. The shape of the nut and the fact that the players run with it under an arm has led to the game being referred to as coconut rugby. There is no kicking – kicking a weighty coconut would be hard enough with a boot but impossible with bare feet and attempting a drop kick would break a lot of naked toes. Nevertheless, the game's long history has led to speculation that it was here in the valleys of northern India that rugby had its beginnings. The idea does not go down well at Rugby School. It was at this public school in Warwickshire in 1823 that during a game of football one William Webb Ellis picked up the ball and ran with it. Far from being admonished for committing a heinous foul, the 16-year-old was credited with inventing rugby and subsequently immortalised in a bronze statue. With a mass of wavy hair, a large knotted handkerchief around his neck and clad in a long-sleeved shirt and flannels and clasping a ball to his stomach, the Ellis bronze statue stands on a plinth outside the school. Which leaves the shirtless, shoeless coconut-carrying rugby players in Manipur little option but to grudgingly acquiesce in their one-time colonial masters retaining ownership of rugby's beginnings. (See p.15 of colour section.)

While animal sacrifice is generally on the decline amongst Hindu communities, it has begun to surface in the most unlikely place imaginable where even the courts have recognised it as integral to the practice of a religion. But it has nothing to do with the Hindu faith. New York has, over the past forty years, seen a steady rise in people practicing Santeria, a syncretic religion that has its home amongst the Yoruba tribe of Nigeria and came to Cuba with the tens of thousands of African slaves that descended on the island towards the end of the eighteenth century. From Cuba, Santeria spread first to Miami and then into the Latino districts of New York. Initiation rites include the sacrifice of chickens, goats and lambs, causing much angst amongst animal rights organisations but winning acceptance at the US Supreme Court which has recognised the killings as a religious sacrament. After initiation, the practice of Santeria outside Nigeria relies heavily on the coconut.

The Yoruba who practice Santeria in Nigeria are a tribe of some 20 million living in the southwest of the country. There they use the kola nut for divine guidance. The nut breaks naturally into four parts and the manner in which the parts end up when tossed on the floor gives the priest, or *Babalawo,* his divine guidance. With the lack of kola nuts in Cuba, the Yoruba slaves turned to coconuts, cutting them into four equal pieces to simulate the kola. And to hide their imported religious practices from their masters, the Africans carefully began to blend their rites and rituals with those of the Catholic Church in whose arms they found themselves.

With Fidel Castro's communist regime closing the churches and causing most of the Catholic priests to flee the country, the practice of Santeria went underground, and stayed there for the best part of his repressive regime. But with Fidel's long illness and final death, the Church began to flourish once again and Santeria came out into the open – albeit a little gingerly to start with. (Rumours that Castro himself was a Santeria follower have been around for years with Santeros claiming to have witnessed his participation in a number of rites and rituals. In 2008 Cuban *Babalawos* were telling foreign reporters that they were practising what was clearly witchcraft to restore Castro to health, and even claimed the ailing communist leader had let them help his cancer-ridden friend, the Venezuelan leader Hugo Chavez.)

In New York, as in Miami and in Cuba, the *Babalawo*'s house serves as home and temple where statues of saints are surrounded by candles and bowls of coconuts. For Miguel De La Torre, an assistant professor of religion at Hope College in Michigan, who was brought up in the Santeria faith, the coconut is 'an object of adoration containing healing, cleansing and divine properties'. The nut aids the *Babalawo* in offering support and guidance over matters of relationships, work, health and financial problems. For it is through the divine guidance gleaned from the coconut that the *Babalawo* communicates with the *orishas*, the demi-gods or spirits. Newly initiated Santeros (those initiated into the Santeria religion) are encouraged to wear white and nothing but white to emphasise their new-found purity.

At the end of the 1990s, Santeria arrived on Broadway in the Paul Simon musical *The Capeman*. Simon, whose songs include 'The Sound of Silence', 'Bridge Over Troubled Water' and 'Mrs Robinson', had teamed up with the Nobel prize-winning poet Derek Walcott to produce a musical based on the life of a convicted murderer-turned-poet. In the show, one of the characters takes her son to a Santero to gain some indication of how the young man's life might turn out. In the orchestra pit, consecrated Bata drums beat out rhythms providing a subtext of Santeria symbolism. But the demi-gods and spirits of Santeria could not prevent the musical from disappointing its audiences, and it closed after just two months. Santeria, on the other hand, was at the beginning of what looked like a long run. With its divine coconuts, it was establishing its presence in the Bronx from where it has spread to the other Latino neighbourhoods across New York, challenging the authorities with some of its extreme rituals and practices as it offers community and divine guidance to impressionable lost souls.

A Santeria initiate wears white in downtown Havana, Cuba.
(© The author)

Set against the 1 billion adherents to the Hindu faith, and even the 20 million who subscribe to Santeria, a following of 3,500 looks modest to say the least. There was, however, nothing modest about the leader of one small but devout group of people. Nguyen Thanh Nam, a diminutive, middle-class, publicity-seeking Vietnamese scholar who had studied chemistry in France, became disillusioned with Western science, exchanged his white lab coat for saffron robes and began preaching an eclectic form of Buddhism from a pagoda floating in the Mekong Delta. His followers regarded him as little short of a saint. In 1969 he had set out from Saigon on a bicycle for Hanoi on a one-man mission to bring the north and south Vietnamese to the peace table. He apparently covered some 300km before being intercepted and sent home with his tail between his legs. At home he took stock and began a new phase of his life, becoming a vegetarian and living on nothing but coconuts. To start with he was known affectionately by his followers as Uncle Hai, but living as he did on nothing but coconuts, he was soon referred to by everyone who knew him as the Coconut Monk.

He came to international prominence when he ran for president of South Vietnam in 1971, promising to end the war within a couple of months. With smiling eyes and wiry silver strands of a goatee beard and wrapped in Buddhist robes, he displayed Christ on an elaborate cross around his neck causing most of the country's electorate to see him as an imposter or at best a mad monk which only invoked unfortunate comparisons with the Romanovs' Rasputin. (Rasputin also enjoyed a frugal diet – in his case fish soup with black bread.) The Coconut Monk made little headway on the mainstream political stage, but his disciples continued to support him as he worked for peace from his colourful pagoda home decorated garishly with Buddhist, Christian and other symbols – a melange described by visitors as Disneyland with religious overtones. One such visitor was John Steinbeck IV, the son of the Nobel laureate. The young Steinbeck had a troubled past and was persuaded by his father to enlist rather than resist the Vietnam draft. He arrived in Saigon in 1965 to work as a correspondent for the US military. His reporting skills would have been muddied by censorship, and colleagues credited him with knowing more of Saigon's bars than anyone else. At the same time he was a serious Buddhist and soon fell under the spell of the Coconut Monk whose pagoda island had become a sanctuary for draft dodgers, deserters and others desperately seeking refuge from the war. The hammering of great bells brought everyone to their knees several times a day to pray for peace. (See p.14 of colour section.)

Steinbeck was back in Vietnam in 1968 after his discharge. With Errol Flynn's son Sean, he founded the Dispatch News Service through which Seymour Hersch cabled his report of the infamous Mi Lai massacre. Steinbeck took Flynn to meet his Coconut Monk and both men enjoyed the calm of the peace pagoda. Believing his mission was to bring an end to the war in Vietnam, the Coconut Monk supervised the building of a grand eight-sided table at which he planned to seat the members of the Joint Military Commission. Negotiation between the hostile parties under his auspices was, he believed, the only way to bring the war to an end. But the commissioners never came. And when the war ended in 1975, the victorious communists disbanded the coconut cult and imprisoned its leader on charges of anti-government activities. The Coconut Monk was put under house arrest and died in unexplained circumstances in 1990 while trying to escape. He was 81.

The coconut cult that developed in the middle of the Mekong Delta during the Vietnam War might have taken inspiration from a rather smaller cult that sprang up a century earlier in what was German New Guinea. 'Come to the South Seas, take your clothes off and eat coconut,' was the invitation issued by a German nudist, vegetarian and sun worshipper by the name of August Engelhardt. It was an invitation that raised a few eyebrows in the rigid Victorian-like society that was Germany at the beginning of the twentieth century.

Kaiser Wilhelm, Queen Victoria's austere and crippled grandson (a difficult breach birth had left him with a stunted left arm) was on the emperor's throne. Just 29 years old and connected to most of Europe's ruling families, Wilhelm's arrogance and lack of tact was soon to be combined with a Teutonic bellicosity and a hunger for power. Engelhardt could not have been more different. Born in Nuremberg, the son of a middle-class factory owner who made paint, he arrived at Erlangen University at the end of the 1890s to study physics and chemistry. A scrawny restless student, whose long and unkempt beard was in stark contrast to the Kaiser's neatly trimmed and waxed moustache, the young August felt decidedly uncomfortable in the Germany the Kaiser was building.

Engelhardt shared his search for an alternative way of life by penning magazine articles advocating radical ways of thinking and living – an end to marriage, an evacuation of towns and cities in favour of a rural existence, and, as God had intended, a return to living without clothes. ('The two basic items necessary to sustain life are sunshine and coconut milk,' mused actor Dustin Hoffman a century later.) A tradition of naturism has developed in Germany where today there are numerous *freikorperkultur* clubs – free body culture clubs which embrace nudity. But this culture of free expression was a long way off in the Germany of the early twentieth century. On graduating, Engelhardt found a job as a pharmacist's assistant where his interest in an alternative lifestyle of healthy eating and natural cures grew into an obsession.

And it was coconuts that would sustain this new way of living – coconuts and plenty of sun. Coconuts, argued Engelhardt, would provide all the nutrition a man needed, and while the fruit would provide food and drink, the tree itself would provide shelter. So with a thousand books for company and a substantial inheritance for financial support, he made his way to Bremen and booked a passage on a mail boat heading for German New Guinea via Singapore. The journey took the better part of three months and Engelhardt finally arrived in the Bismark Archipelago (now Papua New Guinea) in the autumn of 1902. The coconut Camelot of his dreams was at first elusive. He spent frustrating days island-hopping until after several weeks he came upon a tiny coral atoll the locals called Kahakua. He recognised this immediately as his palm temple of pure natural life with its coconut plantations, protected lagoon, dense vegetation groaning with tropical fruits – breadfruits, mango and guava – and nothing but the pounding waves and songs of the birds to break the silence. (There were, he was to discover later, forty Melanesians living on the island.)

He bought a 75-hectare coconut plantation, built a wooden cabin – complete with shelves for his library of books – discarded his clothes and set about collecting supplies of coconuts. To Engelhardt, life soon proved idyllic, so much so that he felt justified in inviting other like-minded cocovore naturists to join him. His aim was not only to establish a fruit and vegetable eating colony of nudists in the South Pacific but to 'girdle the world with a chain of settlements. We will send out missionaries – men who have been tried and found not wanting – to preach our beliefs to all peoples in the lands of the sun.' It was not just his missionaries who would have to be up to scratch: members of his utopian cult were expected to meet a number of demanding criteria. The invitations for people to join him which he sent back to Germany carried a number of conditions. According to a despatch in *The New York Times* from a special correspondent in Sydney published three years after Engelhardt arrived on Kahakua, the eccentric

German was very particular about the men – and it was only men initially – who might join him:

> 'At Kahakua all members of the order must lead a permanent naked life, joining nature in every respect,' he insisted. 'Only men of noble and excellent character will be admitted. Each applicant must be recommended by two respected persons, both known to the leader of the sun-worshippers. A payment of 250 dollars must be made by such applicants as can afford that amount: by less wealthy persons a sum corresponding to their means, and by poor but devout sun-worshippers – nothing.'

With the invitations despatched, Engelhardt settled into a life with his books, swimming, lying in the sun and eating coconuts. The island's Melanesians kept their distance. Being naked themselves they will have sensed they had at least something in common with this strange newcomer.

In time, the ship bringing what he hoped would be the first group of like-minded naturists appeared on the horizon. It made its way slowly towards the island and into the lagoon. Engelhardt stood on the beach, his eyes straining to identify the passengers transferring into the ship's small tender. As it made its way across the still water, it became painfully clear that it carried just four passengers, and two of those were members of the ship's crew. Disappointed by the lack of numbers, Engelhardt was nevertheless delighted with his two new recruits. Heinrich Eukens was a 24-year-old fellow student and vegetarian from Bavaria and Max Lutzow was the celebrated musician from Berlin where a leading orchestra bore his name. Impressed by Engelhardt's physical condition – he was bronzed and appeared in excellent health – the two newcomers immediately joined the routine based on coconuts and plenty of sun. But this sudden change in diet and life in the open did not suit Eukens. He became unwell, developed a fever, lost consciousness and died within days. Lutzow

August Engelhardt (standing) with the Berlin concert pianist Max Lutzow in German New Guinea *c.* 1905.

and Engelhardt buried him in the sand and tried to get on with their lives.

For a while, things improved and Lutzow was soon tanned and energised just like his companion. But this tropical existence had not dulled his love of music. Lutzow's contacts had given him access to one of the first clockwork gramophones and on this he played scratchy and poorly reproduced renderings of his favourite music. But this did not suit Engelhardt who took particular exception to Bizet's *Carmen* and to everything and anything written by Donizetti. The two quarrelled bitterly and Lutzow decided to leave. He slipped away during the night and took refuge on a cutter lying at anchor in the lagoon. But bad weather and strong currents prevented the ship from sailing. Lutzow chose not to take shelter below decks and refused to eat anything that was not fruit. When the fruit ran out, Lutzow starved. Exposed to the wind and continuous rain and rejecting all offers of food, the musician became weak and feverish. His condition grew steadily worse and within a week he had died. Engelhardt buried him in the sand alongside Eukens.

Researchers differ over what happened next. Some accounts suggest that Engelhardt was joined by up to thirty disciples eager to experience what they believed was a utopian existence in the South Seas. Other reports claim Engelhardt continued to live alone until a drought ruined the crop of fruit and coconuts and a storm swept away what was left. Weak and malnourished, his immune system began to fail and he contracted malaria. A trio of local Melanesians found him delirious, talking to the trees. They sent word to the German administrative headquarters at Herbertshohe, some 15 miles away across the water, and a launch with a doctor on board was dispatched to pick him up. He was taken screaming on board and had to be restrained. He refused both nourishment and medicines. Before nightfall he was dead. The launch returned to the lagoon and in the morning Engelhardt's body was wrapped in a German flag and buried alongside Eukens and Lutzow.

Engelhardt's ambition – his naked ambition – to live a life in the sun sustained by coconuts had been thwarted. And the experiment had cost the lives of others too. Napalm, with its palmitic acid, cost the lives of many, many more. But on the whole, the effect of the coconut on mankind has been a benevolent one. Coconut water has become the health drink for millennials. A billion Hindus turn to the coconut for their daily rituals. Consider the many applications of the nut's coir alongside those associated with the charcoal from the shell, and the coconut emerges as the shy solution to all manner of twenty-first-century challenges. Add to this the many peaceful uses of the oil from the nut's white flesh – cooking, candlemaking, soapmaking, lubrication, beauty products, and the tons of desiccated coconut used every day by confectioners and bakers – and you have a plant that has been around for a few thousand years and is still capable of finding new ways of shaping the chaotic world we live in.

Acknowledgements

Many people generously shared their knowledge and experiences in the preparation of this book. Others were generous with their time in various areas of my endeavours. I am enormously grateful to all of them.

Special thanks to Hugh Harries, John Lever of Jacobi Carbons, Rosella Villaruel of the Philippine Coconut Authority, P. Kishore of Malayalam Manorama, Johny Malayil, Christina and Sanitha, Shaji Palathingal, Colin Robson, Andrew Morgan, Robert Pearce at ITER, Francisco Manosa, Greg Peterson of the Edgewood Chemical Biological Centre. My wife Aileen who read and re-read every word, making suggestions and corrections as she did so. And thanks to my editor at The History Press Amy Rigg, whose initial enthusiasm for the book, and subsequent energy in bringing it to fruition, was central to carrying the project through.

Every effort has been made to trace copyright holders and to obtain their permission for the use of copyright material. I apologise for any errors or omissions and would be grateful if notified of any corrections that should be incorporated in future reprints or editions of this book.

BIBLIOGRAPHY

Deeter, Annie, *The Coconut Bible: The Complete Coconut Reference Guide – From Ancient Mariner to Modern Miracle* (Galahad Press, 2014)

Ferguson, John, *All About the Coconut Palm* (Cocos nucifera)*: Including Practical Instructions for Planting and Cultivation* (A.M. & J. Ferguson, 1904)

Knott, Kim, *Hinduism: A Very Short Introduction* (Oxford University Press, 2000)

Pritchard, Andrew with Parker, Norman, *Urban Smuggler* (Mainstream Publishing, 2008)

Swasy, Alecia, *Soap Opera: The Inside Story of Procter & Gamble* (Touchstone, 1993)

Wilson, Charles, *The History of Unilever* (Cassell, 1954)

INDEX

The History Press
The destination for history
www.thehistorypress.co.uk